The Birthday Party

A PLAY IN THREE ACTS

By Harold Pinter

S A M U E L   F R E N C H ,   I N C .

45 WEST 25TH STREET   NEW YORK 10010

7623 SUNSET BOULEVARD   HOLLYWOOD 90046

LONDON   *TORONTO*

THE BIRTHDAY PARTY, by Harold Pinter, directed by Alan Schneider, with setting and costumes by William Ritman, lighting by Tharon Musser, was presented by Haila Stoddard, Mark Wright and Leonard S. Field, Duane Wilder, associate producer, at the Booth Theatre, N.Y.C., October 3, 1967.

CHARACTERS
(In Order of Their Appearance)

PETEY .... *Henderson Forsythe*

MEG .... *Ruth White*

STANLEY .... *James Patterson*

LULU .... *Alexandra Berlin*

GOLDBERG .... *Ed Flanders*

McCANN .... *Edward Winter*

SCENES

The living room of a house in a seaside town in England.

ACT I: *A morning in summer*

ACT II: *Evening of the same day*

ACT III: *The next morning*

The Birthday Party

ACT ONE

The living-room of a house in a seaside town. A door leading to the hall D. L. *Back door and small window* U. L. *Kitchen hatch,* U. C. *Kitchen door* U. R. *Table and chairs,* C.

PETEY *enters from the door* L. *with a paper, hangs his ticket machine and his money pouch on the hook, and sits* L. *of table. He begins to read.* MEG'S *voice comes through the kitchen hatch.*

MEG. Is that you, Petey? (*Pause.*) Petey, is that you? (*Pause.*) Petey?

PETEY. What?

MEG. Is that you?

PETEY. Yes, it's me.

MEG. What? (*Her face appears at the hatch.*) Are you back?

PETEY. Yes.

MEG. I've got your cornflakes ready. (*She disappears and re-appears.*) Here's your cornflakes. (*He rises and takes the plate from her, sits at the table, props up the paper and begins to eat.* MEG *enters by the kitchen door with her tea.*) Are they nice?

PETEY. Very nice.

MEG. I thought they'd be nice. (*She sits* R. *of table.*) You got your paper?

PETEY. Yes.

MEG. Is it good?

PETEY. Not bad.

MEG. What does it say?

PETEY. Nothing much.

MEG. You read me out some nice bits yesterday.

PETEY. Yes, well, I haven't finished this one yet.

MEG. Will you tell me when you come to something good?

PETEY. Yes.

(*Pause.*)

MEG. Have you been working hard this morning?

PETEY. No. Just stacked a few of the old chairs. Cleaned up a bit.

MEG. Is it nice out?

PETEY. Very nice.

(*Pause.*)

MEG. Is Stanley up yet?

PETEY. I don't know. Is he?

MEG. I don't know. I haven't seen him down yet.

PETEY. Well then, he can't be up.

MEG. Haven't you seen him down?

PETEY. I've only just come in.

MEG. He must be still asleep. (*She looks round the room, stands, goes to the sideboard and takes a pair of socks from a drawer, collects wool and a needle and goes back to the table.*) What time did you go out this morning, Petey?

PETEY. Same time as usual.

MEG. Was it dark?

PETEY. No, it was light.

MEG. (*Beginning to darn.*) But sometimes you go out in the morning and it's dark.

PETEY. That's in the winter.

MEG. Oh, in winter.

PETEY. (*Finishes cornflakes and turns paper.*) Yes, it gets light later in winter.

MEG. Oh. (*Pause.*) What are you reading?

PETEY. Someone's just had a baby.

MEG. Oh, they haven't! Who?

PETEY. Some girl.

MEG. Who, Petey, who?

PETEY. I don't think you'd know her.

MEG. What's her name?

PETEY. Lady Mary Splatt.

MEG. I don't know her.

PETEY. No.

MEG. What is it?

PETEY. (*Studying the paper.*) Er—a girl.

MEG. Not a boy?

PETEY. No.

MEG. Oh, what a shame. I'd be sorry. I'd much rather have a little boy.

PETEY. A little girl's all right.

MEG. I'd much rather have a little boy.

PETEY. (*Pause; vaguely.*) I've finished my cornflakes.

MEG. Were they nice?

PETEY. Very nice.

MEG. I've got something else for you. (*She rises, takes his plate and her cup and exits into the kitchen. She then appears at the hatch with two pieces of fried bread on a plate.*)

PETEY. Good.

MEG. Here you are, Petey. (*He rises, collects the plate, looks at it, sits at the table.* MEG *re-enters.*) Is it nice?

PETEY. I haven't tasted it yet.

MEG. I bet you don't know what it is.

PETEY. Yes, I do.

MEG. What is it, then?

PETEY. Fried bread.

MEG. That's right.

(*He begins to eat. She watches him eat.*)

PETEY. Very nice.

MEG. I knew it was. (*She sits.*)

PETEY. (*Turning to her.*) Oh, Meg, two men came up to me on the beach last night.

MEG. Two men?

PETEY. Yes. They wanted to know if we could put them up for a couple of nights.

MEG. Put them up? Here?

PETEY. Yes.

MEG. How many men?

PETEY. Two.

MEG. What did you say?

PETEY. Well, I said I didn't know. So they said they'd come round to find out.

MEG. Are they coming?

PETEY. Well, they said they would.

MEG. Had they heard about us, Petey?

PETEY. They must have done.

MEG. (*She begins to tidy the room.*) Yes, they must have done. They must have heard this was a very good boarding house. It is. This house is on the list.

PETEY. It is.

MEG. I know it is.

PETEY. They might turn up today. Can you do it?

MEG. Oh, I've got that lovely room they can have.

PETEY. You've got a room ready?

MEG. I've got the room with the armchair all ready for visitors.

PETEY. You're sure?

MEG. Yes, that'll be all right then, if they come today.

PETEY. Good. (*Finishes eating.*)

MEG. (*She takes the socks etc. back to the sideboard drawer and starts for the stairs.*) I'm going to wake that boy.

PETEY. There's a new show coming to the Palace.

MEG. On the pier?

PETEY. No. The Palace, in the town.

MEG. Stanley could have been in it, if it was on the pier.

PETEY. This is a straight show.

MEG. What do you mean?

PETEY. No dancing or singing.

MEG. What do they do then?

PETEY. They just talk.

(*Pause.*)

MEG. Oh.

PETEY. You like a song, eh, Meg?

MEG. I like listening to the piano. I used to like watching Stanley play the piano. Of course, he didn't sing. (*Looking at the door.*) I'm going to call that boy.

PETEY. Didn't you take him up his cup of tea?

MEG. I always take him up his cup of tea. But that was a long time ago.

PETEY. Did he drink it?

MEG. I made him. I stood there till he did. I'm going to call him. (*She goes to the foot of the stairs.*) Stan! Stanny! (*She listens.*) Stan! I'm coming up to fetch you if you don't come down! I'm coming up! I'm going to count three! One! Two! Three! I'm coming to get you! (*She exits and goes upstairs. In a moment, shouts from* STANLEY, *wild laughter from* MEG. PETEY *takes his plate to the hatch. Shouts. Laughter.* PETEY *sits at the table. Silence. She returns.*) He's coming down. (*She is panting and arranges her hair.*) I told him if he didn't hurry up he'd get no breakfast.

PETEY. That did it, eh?

MEG. I'll get his cornflakes.

(MEG *exits to the kitchen.* PETEY *reads the paper. DOOR-SLAM upstairs.* STANLEY *enters. He is unshaven, in his pyjama jacket and wears glasses. He sits at the table.*)

PETEY. Morning, Stanley.

STANLEY. Morning.

(*Silence.* MEG *enters with the bowl of cornflakes, which she sets on the table.*)

MEG. So he's come down at last, has he? He's come down at last for his breakfast. But he doesn't deserve any, does he, Petey? (STANLEY *stares at the cornflakes.*) Did you sleep well?

STANLEY. I didn't sleep at all.

MEG. (*Pours milk on cornflakes and tastes them.*) You didn't sleep at all? Did you hear that, Petey? Too tired to eat your breakfast, I suppose? Now you eat up those cornflakes like a good boy. Go on.

STANLEY. (*He begins to eat.*) What's it like out today?

PETEY. Very nice.

STANLEY. Warm?

PETEY. Well, there's a good breeze blowing.

STANLEY. Cold?

PETEY. No, no, I wouldn't say it was cold.

MEG. What are the cornflakes like, Stan?

STANLEY. Horrible.

MEG. Those flakes? Those lovely flakes? You're a liar, a little liar. They're refreshing. It says so. For people when they get up late.

STANLEY. The milk's off.

MEG. It's not. Petey ate his, didn't you, Petey?

PETEY. That's right.

MEG. There you are then.

STANLEY. (*Pushes away his plate.*) All right, I'll go on to the second course.

MEG. He hasn't finished the first course and he wants to go on to the second course!

STANLEY. I feel like something cooked.

MEG. Well, I'm not going to give it to you.

PETEY. Give it to him.

MEG. (*Sitting at the table,* R.) I'm not going to.

(*Pause.*)

STANLEY. No breakfast. (*Pause.*) All night long I've been dreaming about this breakfast.

MEG. I thought you said you didn't sleep.

STANLEY. Day-dreaming. All night long. And now she won't give me any. Not even a crust of bread on the table. (*Pause.*) Well, I can see I'll have to go down to one of those smart hotels on the front.

MEG. (*Rising quickly.*) You won't get a better breakfast there than here. (*She exits to the kitchen with bowl of flakes.* STANLEY *yawns broadly.* MEG *appears at the hatch with a plate.*) Here you are. You'll like this.

(PETEY *rises, collects the plate, brings it to the table, puts it in front of* STANLEY, *and sits.*)

STANLEY. What's this?

PETEY. Fried bread.

MEG. (*Entering.*) Well, I bet you don't know what it is.

STANLEY. Oh, yes I do.

MEG. What?

STANLEY. Fried bread.

MEG. He knew.

STANLEY. What a wonderful surprise.

MEG. You didn't expect that, did you?

STANLEY. I bloody well didn't.

PETEY. (*Puts down his paper and rises.*) Well, I'm off.

MEG. You going back to work?

PETEY. Yes.

MEG. Your tea! You haven't had your tea!

PETEY. That's all right. No time now.

MEG. I've got it made inside.

PETEY. No, never mind. See you later. Ta-ta, Stan.

STANLEY. Ta-ta. (*Reads paper.* PETEY *exits, front door.* MEG *looks after him.*) Tch, tch, tch, tch.

MEG. (*Defensively.*) What do you mean?

STANLEY. You're a bad wife.

MEG. I'm not. Who said I am?

STANLEY. Not to make your husband a cup of tea. Terrible.

MEG. He knows I'm not a bad wife.

STANLEY. Giving him sour milk instead.

MEG. It wasn't sour.

STANLEY. Disgraceful.

MEG. You mind your own business, anyway. (STANLEY *eats.*) You won't find many better wives than me, I can tell you. I keep a very nice house and I keep it clean.

STANLEY. Whoo!

MEG. (*Tidies the window seat.*) Yes! And this house is very well known, for a very good boarding house for visitors.

STANLEY. Visitors? Do you know how many visitors you've had since I've been here?

MEG. How many?

STANLEY. One.

MEG. Who?

STANLEY. Me! I'm your visitor.

MEG. You're a liar. This house is on the list.

STANLEY. I bet it is.

MEG. I know it is. (*He pushes his plate away and picks up the paper. She goes toward him.*) Was it nice?

STANLEY. What?

MEG. The fried bread.

STANLEY. Succulent.

MEG. (*Backs off.*) You shouldn't say that word.

STANLEY. What word?

MEG. That word you said.

STANLEY. What, succulent—?

MEG. Don't say it!

STANLEY. What's the matter with it?

MEG. You shouldn't say that word to a married woman.

STANLEY. Is that a fact?

MEG. Yes.

STANLEY. Well, I never knew that.

MEG. Well, it's true.

STANLEY. Who told you that?

MEG. Never you mind.

STANLEY. Well, if I can't say it to a married woman who can I say it to?

MEG. You're bad.

STANLEY. What about some tea?

MEG. (*Crossing to him.*) Do you want some tea? (STANLEY *reads the paper.*) Say please?

STANLEY. Please.

MEG. Say sorry first.

STANLEY. Sorry first.

MEG. No. Just sorry.

STANLEY. Just sorry!

MEG. You deserve the strap. (*She takes his plate and ruffles his hair as she passes.* STANLEY *exclaims and throws her arm away. She goes into the kitchen. He rubs his eyes under his glasses and picks up the paper. She enters.*) I brought the pot in.

STANLEY. (*Absently.*) I don't know what I'd do without you.

MEG. You don't deserve it, though.

STANLEY. Why not?

MEG. (*Pouring the tea, coyly.*) Go on. Calling me that.

STANLEY. How long has that tea been in the pot?

MEG. It's good tea. Good strong tea.

STANLEY. This isn't tea. It's gravy!

MEG. It's not.

STANLEY. Get out of it. You succulent old washing bag.

MEG. I am not! And it isn't your place to tell me if I am!

STANLEY. And it isn't your place to come into a man's bedroom and—wake him up.

MEG. Stanny! Don't you like your cup of tea of a morning—the one I bring you?

STANLEY. I can't drink this muck. Didn't anyone ever tell you to warm the pot, at least?

MEG. That's good strong tea. That's all.

STANLEY. (*Putting his head in his hands.*) Oh God, I'm tired. (*Silence.* MEG *goes to the sideboard, collects a dust-cloth, and vaguely dusts the sideboard, watching him. She comes to the table and dusts it.*) Not the bloody table!

(*Pause.*)

MEG. Stan?

STANLEY. What?

MEG. (*Shyly.*) Am I really succulent?

STANLEY. Oh, you are. I'd rather have you than a cold in the nose any day.

MEG. You're just saying that.

STANLEY. (*Violently crosses L. and throws himself into the armchair.*) Look, why don't you get this place cleared up! It's a pigsty. And another thing, what about my room? It needs sweeping. It needs papering. I need a new room!

MEG. (*Follows and sits on the arm. Sensual, stroking his arm.*) Oh, Stan, that's a lovely room. I've had some lovely afternoons in that room. (*He recoils from her hand in disgust, stands and exits quickly by door L. She collects his cup and the teapot and takes them to the hatch shelf. The street DOOR SLAMS. STANLEY returns.*) Is the sun shining? (*He crosses to the window, takes a cigarette and matches from his pyjama jacket, and lights his cigarette.*) What are you smoking, Stan?

STANLEY. A cigarette.

MEG. Are you going to give me one?

STANLEY. No.

MEG. I like cigarettes. (*He stands at the window, smoking. She crosses behind him and tickles the back of his neck.*) Tickle, tickle.

STANLEY. (*Pushing her.*) Get away from me. (*Crosses to door R.*)

MEG. Are you going out?

STANLEY. Not with you.

MEG. But I'm going shopping in a minute.

STANLEY. Go.

MEG. You'll be lonely, all by yourself.

STANLEY. Will I?

MEG. Without your old Meg. I've got to get things in for the two gentlemen. (*She goes up to the mirror, takes curlers from her hair, takes off apron and puts on coat and hat*.)

STANLEY. (*He slowly raises his head. He speaks without turning*.) What two gentlemen?

MEG. I'm expecting visitors.

STANLEY. (*He turns*.) What?

MEG. You didn't know that, did you?

STANLEY. What are you talking about?

MEG. Two gentlemen asked Petey if they could come and stay for a couple of nights. I'm expecting them.

STANLEY. I don't believe it.

MEG. It's true.

STANLEY. (*Moving to her*.) You're saying it on purpose.

MEG. Petey told me this morning.

STANLEY. (*Grinding his cigarette*.) When was this? When did he see them?

MEG. Last night.

STANLEY. Who are they?

MEG. I don't know.

STANLEY. Didn't he tell you their names?

MEG. No.

STANLEY. (*Pacing the room*.) Here? They wanted to come here?

MEG. Yes, they did.

STANLEY. Why?

MEG. This house is on the list.

STANLEY. But who are they?

MEG. You'll see when they come.

STANLEY. (*Decisively*.) They won't come.

MEG. Why not?

STANLEY. (*Quickly*.) I tell you they won't come. Why didn't they come last night, if they were coming?

MEG. Perhaps they couldn't find the place in the dark. It's not easy to find in the dark.

STANLEY. They won't come. Someone's taking the Michael. Forget all about it. It's a false alarm. A false alarm. (*He sits* R. *of table*.) Where's my tea?

MEG. (*Crossing to him.*) I took it away. You didn't want it.

STANLEY. What do you mean, you took it away?

MEG. I took it away.

STANLEY. What did you take it away for?

MEG. You didn't want it!

STANLEY. Who said I didn't want it?

MEG. You did!

STANLEY. Who gave you the right to take away my tea?

MEG. You wouldn't drink it.

STANLEY. (*He stares at her. Quietly.*) Who do you think you're talking to?

MEG. (*Uncertainly.*) What?

STANLEY. Come here.

MEG. What do you mean?

STANLEY. Come over here.

MEG. No.

STANLEY. I want to ask you something. (MEG *fidgets nervously. She does not go to him.*) Come on. (*Pause.*) All right. I can ask it from here just as well. (*Deliberately.*) Tell me, Mrs. Boles, when you address yourself to me, do you ever ask yourself who exactly you are talking to? Eh? (*Silence. He groans, his trunk falls forward, his head falls into his hands on the table.*)

MEG. (*In a small voice.*) Didn't you enjoy your breakfast, Stan? (*She approaches the table.*) Stan? When are you going to play the piano again? (STANLEY *grunts.*) Like you used to? (STANLEY *grunts.*) I used to like watching you play the piano. When are you going to play it again? (*Sits* L. *of table.*)

STANLEY. I can't, can I?

MEG. Why not?

STANLEY. I haven't got a piano, have I?

MEG. No, I meant like when you were working. That piano.

STANLEY. Go and do your shopping.

MEG. But you wouldn't have to go away if you got a job, would you? You could play the piano on the pier.

STANLEY. (*He looks at her, then speaks airily.*) I've— er— I've been offered a job, as a matter of fact.

MEG. What?

STANLEY. Yes. I'm considering a job at the moment.

MEG. You're not.

STANLEY. A good one, too. A night club. In Berlin.

MEG. Berlin?

STANLEY. Berlin. A night club. Playing the piano. A fabulous salary. And all expenses.

MEG. How long for?

STANLEY. We don't stay in Berlin. Then we go to Athens.

MEG. How long for?

STANLEY. Yes. Then we pay a flying visit to—er—whatsisname—

MEG. Where?

STANLEY. Constantinople. Zagreb. Vladivostok. It's a round-the-world tour.

MEG. Have you played the piano in those places before?

STANLEY. Played the piano? I've played the piano all over the world. All over the country. (*Pause.*) I once gave a concert.

MEG. A concert?

STANLEY. (*Reflectively.*) Yes. It was a good one, too. They were all there that night. Every single one of them. It was a great success. Yes. A concert. At Lower Edmonton.

MEG. What did you wear?

STANLEY. (*To himself.*) I had a unique touch. Absolutely unique. They came up to me. They came up to me and said they were grateful. Champagne we had that night, the lot. (*Pause.*) My father nearly came down to hear me. Well, I dropped him a card anyway. But I don't think he could make it. No, I—I lost the address, that was it. (*Pause.*) Yes. Lower Edmonton. Then after that,

you know what they did? They carved me up. Carved me
up. It was all arranged, it was all worked out. My next
concert. Somewhere else it was. In winter. I went down
there to play. Then, when I got there, the hall was closed,
the place was shuttered up, not even a caretaker. They'd
locked it up. (*Takes off his glasses and wipes them on his
pyjama jacket.*) A fast one. They pulled a fast one. I'd
like to know who was responsible for that. (*Rises and
crosses L. to window. Bitterly.*) All right, Jack, I can take
a tip. They want me to crawl down on my bended knees.
Well I can take a tip . . . any day of the week. (*He re-
places his glasses, then looks at* MEG.) Look at her.
You're just an old piece of rock cake, aren't you? (*He
crosses to her and looks down at her.*) That's what you
are, aren't you?

MEG. Don't you go away again, Stan. You stay here.
You'll be better off. You stay with your old Meg. (*He
groans and sits in the armchair.*) Aren't you feeling well
this morning, Stan? Did you pay a visit this morning?

(*He stiffens, then lifts himself slowly, turns to face her
and speaks low and meaningfully.*)

STANLEY. Meg. Do you know what?
MEG. What?
STANLEY. Have you heard the latest?
MEG. No.
STANLEY. I'll bet you have.
MEG. I haven't.
STANLEY. Shall I tell you?
MEG. What latest?
STANLEY. You haven't heard it?
MEG. No.
STANLEY. They're coming today.
MEG. Who?
STANLEY. They're coming in a van.
MEG. Who?

STANLEY. And do you know what they've got in that van?

MEG. What?

STANLEY. They've got a wheelbarrow in that van.

MEG. (*Rises. Breathlessly.*) They haven't.

STANLEY. (*Rises.*) Oh yes they have.

MEG. You're a liar. (*Backs away to the door at* R.)

STANLEY. (*Advancing upon her.*) A big wheelbarrow. And when the van stops they wheel it out, and they wheel it up the garden path, and then they knock at the front door.

MEG. They don't.

STANLEY. They're looking for someone.

MEG. They're not.

STANLEY. They're looking for someone. A certain person.

MEG. (*Hoarsely.*) No, they're not!

STANLEY. Shall I tell you who they're looking for?

MEG. No!

STANLEY. You don't want me to tell you?

MEG. You're a liar!

(*A sudden KNOCK on the front door.* MEG *edges past* STANLEY *and collects her shopping bag. Another knock on the door.* MEG *goes out.* STANLEY *sidles to the door and listens.*)

VOICE. Hullo, Mrs. Boles. It's come.

MEG. Oh, has it come?

VOICE. Yes, it's just come.

MEG. What, is that it?

VOICE. Yes. I thought I'd bring it round.

MEG. Is it nice?

VOICE. Very nice. What shall I do with it?

MEG. Well, I don't . . . (*Whispers.*)

VOICE. No, of course not . . . (*Whispers.*)

MEG. All right, but . . . (*Whispers.*)

VOICE. I won't . . . (*Whispers.*) Ta-ta, Mrs. Boles.

(STANLEY *quickly sits at the table. Enter* LULU *with parcel and string bag.*)

LULU. Oh, hullo.

STANLEY. Ay-ay.

LULU. I just want to leave this in here.

STANLEY. Do. (LULU *crosses to the sideboard and puts a solid round parcel upon it.*) That's a bulky object.

LULU. You're not to touch it.

STANLEY. Why would I want to touch it?

LULU. Well, you're not to, anyway. (LULU *walks* D. R.) Why don't you open the door? It's all stuffy in here. (*She opens the* D. R. *doors.*)

STANLEY. (*Rising.*) Stuffy? I disinfected the place this morning.

LULU. (*At the door.*) Oh, that's better. (*Pause. She sits above table, takes out a compact and powders her nose.*)

STANLEY. I think it's going to rain today, what do you think?

LULU. I hope so. You could do with it.

STANLEY. Me? I was in the sea at half past six.

LULU. Were you?

STANLEY. I went right out to the head land and back before breakfast. Don't you believe me?

LULU. (*Offering him the compact.*) Do you want to have a look at your face? (STANLEY *withdraws.*) You could do with a shave, do you know that? Don't you ever go out? (*He does not answer.*) I mean, what do you do, just sit around the house like this all day long? (*Pause.*) Hasn't Mrs. Boles got enough to do without having you under her feet all day long?

STANLEY. I always stand on the table when she sweeps the floor.

LULU. Why don't you have a wash? You look terrible.

STANLEY. A wash wouldn't make any difference. (*He crosses* L., *picks up a magazine and sits in the armchair.*)

LULU. (*Rising.*) Come out and get a bit of air. You depress me, looking like that.

STANLEY. Air? Oh, I don't know about that.

LULU. (*Crosses to him with her string bag.*) It's lovely out. And I've got a few sandwiches.

STANLEY. What sort of sandwiches?

LULU. Cheese.

STANLEY. I'm a big eater, you know.

LULU. That's all right. I'm not hungry.

STANLEY. (*Abruptly.*) How would you like to go away with me?

LULU. Where?

STANLEY. Nowhere. Still, we could go.

LULU. But where could we go?

STANLEY. Nowhere. There's nowhere to go. So we could just go. It wouldn't matter.

LULU. We might as well stay here.

STANLEY. No. It's no good here.

LULU. Well, where else is there?

STANLEY. Nowhere.

LULU. Well, that's a charming proposal. (*Pause.*) Do you have to wear those glasses?

STANLEY. Yes.

LULU. So you're not coming out for a walk?

STANLEY. I can't at the moment.

LULU. You're a bit of a washout, aren't you?

(*She exits,* L. STANLEY *stands. He then goes to the mirror and looks in it. He goes into the kitchen, takes off his glasses and· begins to wash his face. A KNOCK at the front door.* STANLEY *puts on his glasses and comes to the kitchen door. Another KNOCK.* STANLEY *turns out the kitchen LIGHT and exits by the* D. R. *doors. Enter, by the front door,* GOLDBERG *and* MCCANN. MCCANN *carries two suitcases,* GOLDBERG *a briefcase. They halt inside the door, then walk Downstage.* GOLDBERG *and* MCCANN *look round the room.*)

McCANN. Is this it?

GOLDBERG. (*Puts briefcase on table.*) This is it.

McCANN. Are you sure?

GOLDBERG. Sure I'm sure.

McCANN. (*He puts suitcases down below staircase. Pause.*) What now?

GOLDBERG. Don't worry yourself, McCann. Take a seat.

McCANN. What about you?

GOLDBERG. What about me?

McCANN. Are you going to take a seat?

GOLDBERG. We'll both take a seat. (*Sits in the armchair.* McCANN *sits at the table,* L.) Sit back, McCann. Relax. What's the matter with you? I bring you down for a few days to the seaside. Take a holiday. Do yourself a favour. Learn to relax, McCann, or you'll never get anywhere.

McCANN. Ah sure, I do try, Nat.

GOLDBERG. The secret is breathing. Take my tip. It's a well-known fact. Breathe in, breathe out, take a chance, let yourself go, what can you lose? Look at me. When I was an apprentice yet, McCann, every second Friday of the month my Uncle Barney used to take me to the seaside, regular as clockwork. Brighton, Canvey Island, Rottingdean— Uncle Barney wasn't particular. After lunch on Shabbuss we'd go and sit in a couple of deck chairs—you know, the ones with canopies—we'd have a little paddle, we'd watch the tide coming in, going out, the sun coming down—golden days, believe me, McCann. (*Reminiscent.*) Uncle Barney. Of course, he was an impeccable dresser. One of the old school. He had a house just outside Basingstoke at the time. Respected by the whole community. Culture? Don't talk to me about culture. He was an all-round man, what do you mean? He was a cosmopolitan.

McCANN. (*Rises and goes to the window* L.) Hey, Nat . . .

GOLDBERG. (*Reflectively.*) Yes. One of the old school.

McCANN. Nat. How do we know this is the right house?

GOLDBERG. What?

MCCANN. How do we know this is the right house?

GOLDBERG. What makes you think it's the wrong house?

MCCANN. I didn't see a number on the gate.

GOLDBERG. I wasn't looking for a number.

MCCANN. No?

GOLDBERG. (*Settling in the armchair.*) You know one thing Uncle Barney taught me? Uncle Barney taught me that the word of a gentleman is enough. That's why, when I had to go away on business I never carried any money. One of my sons used to come with me. He used to carry a few coppers. For a paper, perhaps, to see how the M.C.C. was getting on overseas. Otherwise my name was good. Besides, I was a very busy man.

MCCANN. (*Crosses and looks out French doors* R.) What about this, Nat? Isn't it about time someone came in?

GOLDBERG. (*Rises.*) McCann, what are you so nervous about? Pull yourself together. Everywhere you go these days it's like a funeral.

MCCANN. That's true.

GOLDBERG. True? Of course it's true. It's more than true. It's a fact.

MCCANN. You may be right.

GOLDBERG. What is it, McCann? You don't trust me like you did in the old days?

MCCANN. (*Sits* R. *of table.*) Sure I trust you, Nat.

GOLDBERG. (*Above table.*) But why is it that before you do a job you're all over the place, and when you're doing the job you're as cool as a whistle?

MCCANN. I don't know, Nat. I'm just all right once I know what I'm doing. When I know what I'm doing, I'm all right.

GOLDBERG. Well, you do it very well.

MCCANN. Thank you, Nat.

GOLDBERG. You know what I said when this job came up? I mean naturally they approached me to take care of it. And you know who I asked for?

McCANN. Who?

GOLDBERG. You.

McCANN. That was very good of you, Nat.

GOLDBERG. (*Crosses above to* R. *of* McCANN.) No, it was nothing. You're a capable man, McCann.

McCANN. That's a great compliment, Nat, coming from a man in your position.

GOLDBERG. (*Crosses below table to* C.) Well, I've got a position, I won't deny it.

McCANN. You certainly have.

GOLDBERG. I would never deny that I had a position.

McCANN. And what a position!

GOLDBERG. (*Crossing to below stairs.*) It's not a thing I would deny.

McCANN. Yes, it's true, you've done a lot for me. I appreciate it.

GOLDBERG. Say no more.

McCANN. You've always been a true Christian.

GOLDBERG. In a way.

McCANN. No, I just thought I'd tell you that I appreciate it.

GOLDBERG. It's unnecessary to recapitulate.

McCANN. You're right there.

GOLDBERG. Quite unnecessary.

(*Pause.* McCANN *leans forward.*)

McCANN. Hey Nat, just one thing . . .

GOLDBERG. What now?

McCANN. This job—no, listen—this job, is it going to be like anything we've ever done before?

GOLDBERG. Tch, tch, tch.

McCANN. No, just tell me that. Just that, and I won't ask any more.

(GOLDBERG *sighs, stands, goes behind the table, ponders, looks at* McCANN, *and then speaks in a quiet, fluent, official tone.*)

GOLDBERG. The main issue is a singular issue and quite distinct from your previous work. Certain elements, however, might well approximate in points of procedure to some of your other activities. All is dependent on the attitude of our subject. At all events, McCann, I can assure you that the assignment will be carried out and the mission accomplished with no excessive aggravation to you or myself. Satisfied?

MCCANN. Sure. Thank you, Nat.

(MEG *enters,* U. C. *with shopping bag of groceries.*)

GOLDBERG. (*Crosses up to her.*) Ah, Mrs. Boles?

MEG. Yes?

GOLDBERG. We spoke to your husband last night. Perhaps he mentioned us? We heard that you kindly let rooms for gentlemen. So I brought my friend along with me. (*He looks at* MCCANN, *who rises.*) We were after a nice place, you understand. So we came to you. I'm Mr. Goldberg and this is Mr. McCann.

MEG. Very pleased to meet you. (*They shake hands.*)

GOLDBERG. We're pleased to meet you, too.

MEG. That's very nice.

GOLDBERG. You're right. How often do you meet someone it's a pleasure to meet?

MCCANN. Never.

GOLDBERG. (*Leads her to the armchair.*) But today it's different. How are you keeping, Mrs. Boles? (*Takes shopping bag and gives it to* MCCANN *who puts it on the table.*)

MEG. Oh, very well, thank you.

GOLDBERG. Yes? Really?

MEG. Oh yes, really.

GOLDBERG. Well, so what do you say? You can manage to put us up, eh, Mrs. Boles?

MEG. Well, it would have been easier last week.

GOLDBERG. Why? How many have you got here at the moment?

MEG. Just one at the moment.

GOLDBERG. Just one?

MEG. Yes. Just one. Until you came.

GOLDBERG. And your husband, of course?

MEG. Yes, but he sleeps with me.

GOLDBERG. What does he do, your husband?

MEG. He's a deck-chair attendant.

GOLDBERG. Oh, very nice.

MEG. Yes, he's out in all weathers. (*Rises, crosses to table. She begins to take her purchases from her bag.*)

GOLDBERG. Of course. And your guest? Is he a man?

MEG. A man?

GOLDBERG. Or a woman?

MEG. No. A man. (*Goes to kitchen with packages and turns on LIGHT.*)

GOLDBERG. Been here long?

MEG. He's been here about a year now.

GOLDBERG. Oh, yes. A resident. What's his name?

MEG. Stanley Webber.

GOLDBERG. Oh, yes? Does he work here?

MEG. (*Enters from the kitchen.*) He used to work. He used to be a pianist. In a concert party on the pier.

GOLDBERG. Oh, yes? On the pier, eh? Does he play a nice piano?

MEG. Oh, lovely. (*She sits at the table.*) He once gave a concert.

GOLDBERG. Oh? Where?

(GOLDBERG *and* MCCANN *sit at the table.* GOLDBERG *is on her* R.)

MEG. (*Falteringly.*) In . . . a big hall. His father gave him champagne. But then they locked the place up and he couldn't get out. The caretaker had gone home. So he had to wait until the morning before he could get out. (*With confidence.*) They were very grateful. (*Pause.*) And then they all wanted to give him a tip. And so he took the tip. And then he got a fast train and he came down here.

GOLDBERG. Really?

MEG. Oh, yes. Straight down. (MCCANN *rises and crosses to window* L. *Pause.*) I wish he could have played tonight.

GOLDBERG. Why tonight?

MEG. It's his birthday today.

GOLDBERG. His birthday?

MEG. Yes. Today. But I'm not going to tell him until tonight.

GOLDBERG. Doesn't he know it's his birthday?

MEG. He hasn't mentioned it.

GOLDBERG. (*Thoughtfully.*) Well, well, well. Tell me. Are you going to have a party?

MEG. Party?

GOLDBERG. Weren't you going to have one?

MEG. (*Her eyes wide.*) No.

GOLDBERG. Well, of course, you must have one. (*He stands.*) We'll have a party, eh? What do you say?

MEG. Oh, yes!

GOLDBERG. (*Crossing below table to* C.) Sure. We'll give him a party. Leave it to me.

MEG. (*Rises.*) Oh, that's wonderful, Mr. Gold—

GOLDBERG. Berg.

MEG. Berg.

GOLDBERG. You like the idea?

MEG. Oh, I'm so glad you came today.

GOLDBERG. If we hadn't come today we'd have come tomorrow. Still, I'm glad we came today. Just in time for his birthday.

MEG. I wanted to have a party. But you must have people for a party.

GOLDBERG. And now you've got McCann and me. McCann's the life and soul of any party.

MCCANN. What?

GOLDBERG. (*Crosses to him.*) What do you think of that, McCann? There's a gentleman living here. He's got a birthday today, and he's forgotten all about it. So we're going to remind him. We're going to give him a party.

McCANN. Oh, is that a fact?

MEG. Tonight.

GOLDBERG. Tonight.

MEG. I'll put on my party dress.

GOLDBERG. And I'll get some bottles.

MEG. And I'll invite Lulu this afternoon. Oh, this is going to cheer Stanley up. It will. He's been down in the dumps lately.

GOLDBERG. We'll bring him out of himself.

MEG. I hope I look nice in my dress.

GOLDBERG. Madam, you'll look like a tulip.

MEG. What colour?

GOLDBERG. Er—well, I'll have to see the dress first.

McCANN. (*Picks up suitcases.*) Could I go up to my room?

MEG. Oh, I've put you both together. Do you mind being both together?

GOLDBERG. I don't mind. Do you mind, McCann?

McCANN. No.

MEG. What time shall we have the party?

GOLDBERG. Nine o'clock. (*Picks up his briefcase from the table.*)

McCANN. (*On the steps.*) Is this the way?

MEG. (*Rising.*) I'll show you. If you don't mind coming upstairs.

GOLDBERG. With a tulip? It's a pleasure.

(MEG *and* GOLDBERG *exit laughing, followed by* McCANN. STANLEY *appears at the doors* L. *He enters and goes to the stairs and listens. Silence. He walks to the table. He stands. He sits, as* MEG *enters. She crosses to the window seat* L. *He lights a match and watches it burn.*)

STANLEY. Who is it?

MEG. The two gentlemen.

STANLEY. What two gentlemen?

MEG. The ones that were coming. I just took them to their room. They were thrilled with their room.

STANLEY. They've come?

MEG. They're very nice, Stan.

STANLEY. Why didn't they come last night?

MEG. They said the beds were wonderful.

STANLEY. Who are they?

MEG. (*Crosses to him at table.*) They're very nice, Stanley.

STANLEY. I said, who are they?

MEG. I've told you, the two gentlemen.

STANLEY. I didn't think they'd come.

MEG. They have. They were here when I came in.

STANLEY. What do they want here?

MEG. They want to stay.

STANLEY. How long for?

MEG. They didn't say.

STANLEY. (*Rises to* D. R.) But why here? Why not somewhere else?

MEG. This house is on the list. (*Rises, crosses* L. *and arranges cushions on chair.*)

STANLEY. (*Coming down.*) What are they called? What are their names?

MEG. Oh, Stanley, I can't remember.

STANLEY. They told you, didn't they? Or didn't they tell you?

MEG. Yes, they—

STANLEY. Then what are they? Come on. Try to remember.

MEG. Why, Stan? Do you know them?

STANLEY. How do I know if I know them until I know their names?

MEG. (*Crosses below to sideboard.*) Well . . . he told me, I remember.

STANLEY. Well?

MEG. (*She thinks.*) Gold—something.

STANLEY. Goldsomething?

MEG. Yes. Gold . . .

STANLEY. Yes?

MEG. Goldberg.

STANLEY. Goldberg?

MEG. That's right. That was one of them. (*Puts away dustcloth.* STANLEY *slowly sits at the table,* L.) Do you know them? (STANLEY *does not answer.*) Stan, they won't wake you up, I promise. I'll tell them they must be quiet. (STANLEY *sits still.*) They won't be here long, Stan. I'll still bring you up your early morning tea. (STANLEY *sits still.*) You mustn't be sad today. It's your birthday.

(*A pause.*)

STANLEY. (*Dumbly.*) Uh?

MEG. It's your birthday, Stan. I was going to keep it a secret until tonight.

STANLEY. No.

MEG. It is. I've brought you a present. (*She goes to the sideboard, picks up the parcel, and places it on the table in front of him.*) Here. Go on. Open it.

STANLEY. What's this?

MEG. It's your present.

STANLEY. This isn't my birthday, Meg.

MEG. Of course it is. Open your present. (*Sits* R. *of table.*)

STANLEY. (*He stares at the parcel, slowly stands, and opens it. He takes out a boy's drum. Flatly.*) It's a drum. A boy's drum.

MEG. (*Tenderly.*) It's because you haven't got a piano. (*He stares at her, then turns and walks towards the door,* U. C.) Aren't you going to give me a kiss? (*He turns sharply, and stops. He walks back towards her slowly. He stops at her chair, looking down upon her. Pause. His shoulders sag, he bends and kisses her on the cheek.*) There are some sticks in there.

STANLEY. (*He looks into the parcel. He takes out two*

drumsticks. He taps them together. He looks at her.)
Shall I put it round my neck?

(*She watches him, uncertainly. He hangs the drum around
his neck, taps it gently with the sticks, then marches
round the table, beating it regularly. MEG, pleased,
watches him. Still beating it regularly, he begins to
go round the table a second time. Halfway round the
beat becomes erratic, uncontrolled. MEG expresses
dismay. He arrives at her chair, banging the drum,
his face and the drumbeat now savage and pos-
sessed.*)

CURTAIN

ACT TWO

McCann *is sitting at the table tearing a sheet of newspaper into five equal strips. It is evening. After a few moments* STANLEY *enters from* L. *He stops upon seeing* McCann, *and watches him. He then walks toward the kitchen, stops, and speaks.*

STANLEY. Evening.
McCann. Evening.

(*CHUCKLES are heard from outside the doors* D. R., *which are open.*)

STANLEY. Very warm tonight. (*He crosses to doors* D. R. *and looks out.*) Someone out there?

(McCann *tears another length of paper.* STANLEY *goes into the kitchen, turns on the LIGHT and pours a glass of water.* McCann *rises and crosses* U. C. *He drinks it looking through the hatch. He puts the glass down, comes out of the kitchen and walks quickly towards the door,* U. C. McCann *is there.*)

McCann. I don't think we've met.
STANLEY. No, we haven't.
McCann. My name's McCann.
STANLEY. Staying here long?
McCann. Not long. What's your name?
STANLEY. Webber.
McCann. I'm glad to meet you, sir. (*He offers his hand.* STANLEY *takes it, and* McCann *holds the grip.*) Many happy returns of the day. (STANLEY *withdraws his hand. They face each other.*) Were you going out?
STANLEY. Yes.

McCann. On your birthday?

Stanley. Yes. Why not?

McCann. But they're holding a party here for you tonight.

Stanley. Oh, really? That's unfortunate.

McCann. Ah, no. It's very nice.

(*VOICES from outside the back door.*)

Stanley. I'm sorry. I'm not in the mood for a party tonight.

McCann. Oh, is that so? I'm sorry.

Stanley. Yes, I'm going out to celebrate quietly, on my own.

McCann. That's a shame.

(*They stand.*)

Stanley. Well, if you'd move out of my way—

McCann. But everything's laid on. The guests are expected.

Stanley. Guests? What guests?

McCann. Myself for one. I had the honour of an invitation.

Stanley. (*Moving away to* D. R.) I wouldn't call it an honour, would you? It'll just be another booze-up.

McCann. But it is an honour.

Stanley. I'd say you were exaggerating.

McCann. Oh, no. I'd say it was an honour.

Stanley. I'd say that was plain stupid.

McCann. Oh, no.

(*They stare at each other.*)

Stanley. (*Crossing below table to* L.) Who are the other guests?

McCann. A young lady.

Stanley. Oh, yes? And . . . ?

McCANN. My friend.

STANLEY. Your friend?

McCANN. That's right. It's all laid on.

(STANLEY *walks towards the door.* McCANN *meets him.*)

STANLEY. Excuse me.

McCANN. Where are you going?

STANLEY. I want to go out.

McCANN. Why don't you stay here?

(STANLEY *moves away, to* R. *of the table.*)

STANLEY. So you're down here on holiday?

McCANN. A short one. (STANLEY *picks up a strip of paper.* McCANN *moves in.*) Mind that.

STANLEY. What is it?

McCANN. Mind it. Leave it.

STANLEY. I've got a feeling we've met before.

McCANN. No, we haven't.

STANLEY. Ever been anywhere near Maidenhead?

McCANN. No.

STANLEY. There's a Fuller's teashop. I used to have my tea there.

McCANN. (*Sits* L. *of table.*) I don't know it.

STANLEY. And a Boots Library. I seem to connect you with the High Street.

McCANN. Yes?

STANLEY. A charming town, don't you think?

McCANN. I don't know it.

STANLEY. Oh, no. A quiet, thriving community. I was born and brought up there. I lived well away from the main road.

McCANN. Yes?

(*Pause.*)

STANLEY. You're here on a short stay?

MCCANN. That's right.

STANLEY. You'll find it very bracing.

MCCANN. Do you find it bracing?

STANLEY. Me? No. But you will. (*He sits at the table* c.) I like it here, but I'll be moving soon. Back home. I'll stay there too, this time. No place like home. (*He laughs.*) I wouldn't have left, but business calls. Business called, and I had to leave for a bit. You know how it is.

MCCANN. You in business?

STANLEY. No. I think I'll give it up. I've got a small private income, you see. I think I'll give it up. Don't like being away from home. I used to live very quietly—play records, that's about all. Everything delivered to the door. Then I started a little private business, in a small way, and it compelled me to come down here—kept me longer than I expected. You never get used to living in someone else's house. Don't you agree? I lived so quietly. You can only appreciate what you've had when things change. That's what they say, isn't it? Cigarette?

MCCANN. I don't smoke.

(STANLEY *lights a cigarette. VOICES from the back.*)

STANLEY. (*Crosses to doors* R.) Who's out there?

MCCANN. My friend and the man of the house.

STANLEY. (*Crossing in to the table.*) You know what? To look at me, I bet you wouldn't think I'd led such a quiet life. The lines on my face, eh? It's the drink. Been drinking a bit down here. But what I mean is . . . you know how it is . . . away from your own . . . all wrong, of course . . . I'll be all right when I get back . . . but what I mean is, the way some people look at me you'd think I was a different person. I suppose I have changed, but I'm still the same man that I always was. I mean, you wouldn't think, to look at me, really . . . I mean, not really, that I was the sort of bloke to—to cause any

trouble, would you? (McCANN *looks at him.*) Do you
know what I mean?

McCANN. No. (*As* STANLEY *picks up a strip of paper.*)
Mind that.

STANLEY. (*Quickly.*) Why are you down here?

McCANN. A short holiday.

STANLEY. (*Crosses to window* L.) This is a ridiculous
house to pick on.

McCANN. Why?

STANLEY. Because it's not a boarding house. It never
was.

McCANN. Sure it is.

STANLEY. Why did you choose this house?

McCANN. You know, sir, you're a bit depressed for a
man on his birthday.

STANLEY. (*Sharply.*) Why do you call me sir?

McCANN. You don't like it?

STANLEY. (*To the table.*) Listen. Don't call me sir.

McCANN. I won't, if you don't like it.

STANLEY. (*Moving away to French doors.*) No. Anyway, this isn't my birthday.

McCANN. No?

STANLEY. No. It's not till next month.

McCANN. Not according to the lady.

STANLEY. (*Turns.*) Her? She's crazy. Round the bend.

McCANN. That's a terrible thing to say.

STANLEY. (*To the table.*) Haven't you found that out
yet? There's a lot you don't know. I think someone's leading you up the garden path.

McCANN. Who would do that?

STANLEY. (*Leaning across the table.*) That woman is
mad!

McCANN. That's slander.

STANLEY. And you don't know what you're doing.

McCANN. Your cigarette is near that paper.

(*VOICES from the back.*)

STANLEY. Where the hell are they? (*Stubbing his cigarette.*) Why don't they come in? What are they doing out there?

McCANN. You want to steady yourself. (STANLEY *crosses to him and grips his arm.*)

STANLEY. (*Urgently.*) Look—

McCANN. Don't touch me.

STANLEY. Look. Listen a minute.

McCANN. (*Rises.*) Let go of my arm.

STANLEY. Look. Sit down a minute.

McCANN. (*Savagely, hitting him in the stomach.*) Don't do that!

STANLEY. (*He falls to the floor and crawls R. of table.*) Listen. You knew what I was talking about before, didn't you?

McCANN. (*Sits again.*) I don't know what you're at at all.

STANLEY. It's a mistake! Do you understand?

McCANN. You're in a bad state, man.

STANLEY. (*Whispering, advancing.*) Has he told you anything? Do you know what you're here for? Tell me. You needn't be frightened of me. Or hasn't he told you?

McCANN. Told me what?

STANLEY. (*Hissing.*) I've explained to you, damn you, that all those years I lived in Basingstoke I never stepped outside the door.

McCANN. You know, I'm flabbergasted with you.

STANLEY. (*Sits above table. Reasonably.*) Look. You look an honest man. You're being made a fool of, that's all. You understand? Where do you come from?

McCANN. Where do you think?

STANLEY. I know Ireland very well. I've many friends there. I love that country and I admire and trust its people. I trust them. They respect the truth and they have a sense of humour. I think their policemen are wonderful. I've been there. I've never seen such sunsets. What about coming out to have a drink with me? There's a pub down

the road serves draught Guinness. Very difficult to get in
these parts—

(*He breaks off. The voices draw nearer.* GOLDBERG *and*
PETEY *enter from the back door.*)

GOLDBERG. (*As he enters, carrying his jacket.*) A
mother in a million. (*He sees* STANLEY.) Ah.

PETEY. Oh hullo, Stan. You haven't met Stanley, have
you, Mr. Goldberg?

GOLDBERG. I haven't had the pleasure.

PETEY. Oh well, this is Mr. Goldberg, this is Mr.
Webber.

GOLDBERG. Pleased to meet you.

(STANLEY *turns away and crosses* L. *to window seat.*)

PETEY. We were just getting a bit of air in the garden.

GOLDBERG. (*Drapes jacket on back of* C. *chair above
table.*) I was telling Mr. Boles about my old mum. What
days. (PETEY *sits at the table,* R.) Yes. When I was a
youngster, of a Friday, I used to go for a walk down the
canal with a girl who lived down my road. A beautiful
girl. What a voice that bird had! A nightingale, my word
of honour. Good? Pure? She wasn't a Sunday school
teacher for nothing. Anyway, I'd leave her with a little
kiss on the cheek—I never took liberties—we weren't like
the young men these days in those days. We knew the
meaning of respect. So I'd give her a peck and I'd bowl
back home. Humming away I'd be, past the children's
playground. I'd tip my hat to the toddlers, I'd give a
helping hand to a couple of stray dogs, everything came
natural. I can see it like it was yesterday. The sun falling
behind the dog stadium. Ah! (*He leans back con-
tentedly.*)

MCCANN. Like behind the town hall.

GOLDBERG. What town hall?

MCCANN. In Carrikmacross.

GOLDBERG. There's no comparison. Up the street, into my gate, inside the door, home. "Simey!" my old mum used to shout. "Quick before it gets cold." And there on the table what would I see? The nicest piece of gefilte fish you could wish to find on a plate.

McCANN. I thought your name was Nat.

GOLDBERG. She called me Simey.

PETEY. Yes, we all remember our childhood.

GOLDBERG. (*Crosses to* STANLEY.) Too true. Eh, Mr. Webber, what do you say? Childhood. Hot water bottles. Hot milk. Pancakes. Soap suds. What a life.

(*Pause.*)

PETEY. (*Rising from the table.*) Well, I'll have to be off.

GOLDBERG. Off?

PETEY. It's my chess night. (*Crosses* U. C. *for cap and sweater.*)

GOLDBERG. You're not staying for the party?

PETEY. (*Crosses to* STANLEY.) No, I'm sorry, Stan. I didn't know about it till just now. And we've got a game on. I'll try to get back early.

GOLDBERG. We'll save some drink for you, all right? Oh, that reminds me. You'd better go and collect the bottles.

McCANN. Now?

GOLDBERG. Of course, now. Time's getting on. Round the corner, remember? Mention my name.

PETEY. I'm coming your way.

GOLDBERG. Beat him quick and come back, Mr. Boles.

PETEY. Do my best. See you later, Stan.

(PETEY *and* McCANN *go out,* U. C. STANLEY *moves to* C.)

GOLDBERG. A warm night.

STANLEY. (*Turning.*) Don't mess me about!

GOLDBERG. I beg your pardon?

STANLEY. (*Moving Downstage. Gives* GOLDBERG *his*

jacket, puts ashtray on sideboard and moves chairs in at the table.) I'm afraid there's been a mistake. We're booked out. Your room is taken. Mrs. Boles forgot to tell you. You'll have to find somewhere else.

GOLDBERG. (*Puts on his jacket.*) Are you the manager here?

STANLEY. That's right.

GOLDBERG. Is it a good game?

STANLEY. I run the house. I'm afraid you and your friend will have to find other accommodation.

GOLDBERG. (*Crossing Downstage.*) Oh, I forgot, I must congratulate you on your birthday. (*Offering his hand.*) Congratulations.

STANLEY. (*Ignoring hand.*) Perhaps you're deaf?

GOLDBERG. No, what makes you think that? As a matter of fact, every single one of my senses is at its peak. Not bad going, eh? For a man past fifty. (*Sits L. of table.*) But a birthday, I always feel, is a great occasion, taken too much for granted these days. What a thing to celebrate—birth! Like getting up in the morning. Marvelous! Some people don't like the idea of getting up in the morning. I've heard them. Getting up in the morning, they say, what is it? Your skin's crabby, you need a shave, your eyes are full of muck, your mouth is like a boghouse, the palms of your hands are full of sweat, your nose clogged up, your feet stink, what are you but a corpse waiting to be washed? Whenever I hear that point of view I feel cheerful. Because I know what it is to wake up with the sun shining, to the sound of the lawnmower, all the little birds, the smell of the grass, church bells, tomato juice—

STANLEY. Get out. (*Enter* McCANN, *with bottles.*) Get that drink out. These are unlicensed premises.

GOLDBERG. You're in a terrible humour today, Mr. Webber. And on your birthday too, with the good lady getting her strength up to give you a party.

(McCANN *puts the bottles on the sideboard.*)

STANLEY. I told you to get those bottles out.

GOLDBERG. Mr. Webber, sit down a minute.

STANLEY. (*Crosses to* GOLDBERG *at table*.) Let me—just make this clear. You don't bother me. To me, you're nothing but a dirty joke. But I have a responsibility towards the people in this house. They've been down here too long. They've lost their sense of smell. I haven't. And nobody's going to take advantage of them while I'm here. (*A little less forceful*.) Anyway, this house isn't your cup of tea. There's nothing here for you, from any angle. So why don't you just go, without any more fuss?

GOLDBERG. Mr. Webber, sit down.

STANLEY. It's no good starting any kind of trouble.

GOLDBERG. Sit down.

STANLEY. Why should I?

GOLDBERG. If you want to know the truth, Webber, you're beginning to get on my breasts.

STANLEY. (*Crosses to doors* R.) Really? Well, that's—

GOLDBERG. Sit down.

STANLEY. No.

(GOLDBERG *sighs, rises, crosses* L. *and sits at the window seat*.)

GOLDBERG. McCann.

McCANN. Nat?

GOLDBERG. Ask him to sit down.

McCANN. Yes, Nat. (McCANN *moves to* STANLEY.) Do you mind sitting down?

STANLEY. Yes, I do mind.

McCANN. Yes now, but—it'd be better if you did.

STANLEY. Why don't you sit down?

McCANN. No, not me—you.

STANLEY. No thanks.

(*Pause.*)

McCANN. (*He crosses to* GOLDBERG.) Nat.

GOLDBERG. What?
McCANN. He won't sit down.
GOLDBERG. Well, ask him.
McCANN. I've asked him.
GOLDBERG. Ask him again.
McCANN. (*To* STANLEY.) Sit down.
STANLEY. Why?
McCANN. You'de be more comfortable.
STANLEY. So would you.

(*Pause.*)

McCANN. All right. If you will I will.

(*They move to the table,* STANLEY *at* R., McCANN *at* L.)

STANLEY. You first.

(McCANN *slowly sits at the table.* L.)

McCANN. Well?
STANLEY. Right. Now you've both had a rest you can get out!
McCANN. (*Rising.*) That's a dirty trick! I'll kick the shite out of him.
GOLDBERG. (*Rising.*) No! I have stood up.
McCANN. Sit down again!
GOLDBERG. Once I'm up I'm up.
STANLEY. Same here. (*Retreats above table to below stairs.*)
McCANN. (*Following to* STANLEY.) You've made Mr. Goldberg stand up.
STANLEY. (*His voice rising.*) It'll do him good!
McCANN. Get in that seat.
GOLDBERG. McCann.
McCANN. Get down in that seat!
GOLDBERG. (*Crossing to him.*) Webber. (*Quietly.*) SIT DOWN.

(*Silence.* STANLEY *strolls casually to the chair at the
table. They watch him. Silence. He sits. He lights a
cigarette.* MCCANN *crosses behind him, takes cigarette and puts it out in ashtray.*)

STANLEY. (L. *of table.*) You'd better be careful.

GOLDBERG. (*Below landing.*) Webber, what were you
doing yesterday?

STANLEY. Yesterday?

GOLDBERG. And the day before. What did you do the
day before that?

STANLEY. What do you mean?

GOLDBERG. Why are you wasting everybody's time,
Webber? Why are you getting in everybody's way?

STANLEY. Me? What are you—

GOLDBERG. I'm telling you, Webber. You're a washout.
Why are you getting on everybody's wick? Why are you
driving that old lady off her conk?

MCCANN. (*Above* R. *of table.*) He likes to do it!

GOLDBERG. Why do you behave so badly, Webber?
Why do you force that old man out to play chess?

STANLEY. Me?

GOLDBERG. Why do you treat that young lady like a
leper? She's not the leper, Webber!

STANLEY. What the—

GOLDBERG. What did you wear last week, Webber?
Where do you keep your suits?

MCCANN. Why did you leave the organization?

GOLDBERG. What would your old mum say, Webber?

MCCANN. Why did you betray us?

GOLDBERG. You hurt me, Webber. You're playing a
dirty game.

(*They close in on him.*)

MCCANN. That's a Black and Tan fact.

GOLDBERG. Who does he think he is?

MCCANN. Who do you think you are?

STANLEY. You're on the wrong horse.

GOLDBERG. When did you come to this place?

STANLEY. Last year.

GOLDBERG. Where did you come from?

STANLEY. Somewhere else.

GOLDBERG. Why did you come here?

STANLEY. My feet hurt!

GOLDBERG. Why did you stay?

STANLEY. I had a headache!

GOLDBERG. Did you take anything for it?

STANLEY. Yes.

GOLDBERG. What?

STANLEY. Fruit salts!

GOLDBERG. Enos or Andrews?

STANLEY. En— An—

GOLDBERG. Did you stir properly? Did they fizz?

STANLEY. Now, now, wait, you—

GOLDBERG. Did they fizz? Did they fizz or didn't they fizz?

McCANN. He doesn't know!

GOLDBERG. You don't know. When did you last have a bath?

STANLEY. I have one every—

GOLDBERG. Don't lie.

McCANN. You betrayed the organization. I know him!

STANLEY. You don't!

GOLDBERG. What can you see without your glasses?

STANLEY. Anything.

GOLDBERG. Take off his glasses. (McCANN *snatches his glasses and as* STANLEY *rises, reaching for them, takes his chair* D. C., *below the table,* STANLEY *stumbling as he follows.* STANLEY *clutches the chair and sits on it facing Upstage.*) Webber, you're a fake. (*They stand on each side of the chair.*) When did you last wash up a cup?

STANLEY. The Christmas before last.

GOLDBERG. Where?

STANLEY. Lyons Corner House.

GOLDBERG. Which one?

STANLEY. Marble Arch.

GOLDBERG. Where was your wife?

STANLEY. In—

GOLDBERG. Answer.

STANLEY. (*Turning, crouched.*) What wife?

GOLDBERG. What have you done with your wife?

McCANN. He's killed his wife!

GOLDBERG. Why did you kill your wife?

STANLEY. (*Sitting, his back to the audience.*) What wife?

McCANN. How did he kill her?

GOLDBERG. How did you kill her?

McCANN. You throttled her.

GOLDBERG. With arsenic.

McCANN. There's your man!

GOLDBERG. Where's your old mum?

STANLEY. In the sanatorium.

McCANN. Yes!

GOLDBERG. Why did you never get married?

McCANN. She was waiting at the porch.

GOLDBERG. You skedaddled from the wedding.

McCANN. He left her in the lurch.

GOLDBERG. You left her in the pudding club.

McCANN. She was waiting at the church.

GOLDBERG. Webber! Why did you change your name?

STANLEY. I forgot the other one.

GOLDBERG. What's your name now?

STANLEY. Joe Soap.

GOLDBERG. You stink of sin.

McCANN. I can smell it.

GOLDBERG. Do you recognise an external force?

STANLEY. What?

GOLDBERG. Do you recognise an external force?

McCANN. That's the question!

GOLDBERG. Do you recognise an external force, responsible for you, suffering for you?

STANLEY. (*Starting up.*) It's late.

GOLDBERG. (*Pushes him down.*) Late! Late enough! When did you last pray?

McCANN. He's sweating!

GOLDBERG. When did you last pray?

McCANN. He's sweating!

GOLDBERG. Is the number 846 possible or necessary?

STANLEY. Neither.

GOLDBERG. Wrong! Is the number 846 possible or necessary?

STANLEY. Both.

GOLDBERG. Wrong! It's necessary but not possible.

STANLEY. Both.

GOLDBERG. Wrong! Why do you think the number 846 is necessarily possible?

STANLEY. Must be.

GOLDBERG. Wrong! It's only necessarily necessary! We admit possibility only after we grant necessity. It is possible because necessary but by no means necessary through possibility. The possibility can only be assumed after the proof of necessity.

McCANN. Right!

GOLDBERG. Right? Of course right! We're right and you're wrong, Webber, all along the line.

McCANN. All along the line!

GOLDBERG. Where is your lechery leading you?

McCANN. You'll pay for this.

GOLDBERG. You stuff yourself with dry toast.

McCANN. You contaminate womankind.

GOLDBERG. Why don't you pay the rent?

McCANN. Mother defiler!

GOLDBERG. Why do you pick your nose?

McCANN. I demand justice!

GOLDBERG. What's your trade?

McCANN. What about Ireland?

GOLDBERG. What's your trade?

STANLEY. I play the piano.

GOLDBERG. How many fingers do you use?

STANLEY. No hands!

GOLDBERG. No society would touch you. Not even a building society.

McCANN. You're a traitor to the cloth.

GOLDBERG. What do you use for pyjamas?

STANLEY. Nothing.

GOLDBERG. You verminate the sheet of your birth.

McCANN. What about the Albigensist heresy?

GOLDBERG. Who watered the wicket in Melbourne?

McCANN. What about the blessed Oliver Plunkett?

GOLDBERG. Speak up, Webber. Why did the chicken cross the road?

STANLEY. He wanted to—he wanted to—he wanted to . . .

McCANN. He doesn't know!

GOLDBERG. Why did the chicken cross the road?

STANLEY. He wanted to—he wanted to . . .

GOLDBERG. Why did the chicken cross the road?

STANLEY. He wanted . . .

McCANN. He doesn't know. He doesn't know which came first!

GOLDBERG. Which came first?

McCANN. Chicken? Egg? Which came first?

GOLDBERG and McCANN. Which came first? Which came first? Which came first?

(STANLEY *screams*.)

GOLDBERG. He doesn't know. Do you know your own face?

McCANN. Wake him up. Stick a needle in his eye.

GOLDBERG. You're a plague, Webber. You're an overthrow.

McCANN. You're what's left!

GOLDBERG. But we've got the answer to you. We can sterilise you.

McCANN. What about Drogheda?

GOLDBERG. Your bite is dead. Only your pong is left.

McCANN. You betrayed our land.

GOLDBERG. You betray our breed.

MCCANN. Who are you, Webber?

GOLDBERG. What makes you think you exist?

MCCANN. You're dead.

GOLDBERG. You're dead. You can't live, you can't think, you can't love. You're dead. You're a plague gone bad. There's no juice in you. You're nothing but an odour! (*Silence. They stand over him. He is crouched in the chair. He looks up slowly and kicks* GOLDBERG *in the stomach.* GOLDBERG *falls.* STANLEY *stands.* MCCANN *seizes a chair and lifts it above his head.* STANLEY *seizes a stool and covers his head with it.* MCCANN *and* STANLEY *circle the table from* U. L. *to* D. R.) Steady, McCann.

STANLEY. (*Circling.*) Uuuuuhhhhh!

MCCANN. Right, Judas.

GOLDBERG. (*Rising.*) Steady, McCann.

MCCANN. Come on!

STANLEY. Uuuuuuuuhhhhh!

MCCANN. He's sweating.

GOLDBERG. Easy, McCann.

MCCANN. The bastard sweatpig is sweating.

(*A loud DRUMBEAT off* L. STANLEY *drops stool and crosses to window seat. They put the chairs down. They stop still. Enter* MEG, *in evening dress, holding sticks and drum.*)

MEG. I brought the drum down. I'm dressed for the party.

GOLDBERG. Wonderful.

MEG. You like my dress?

GOLDBERG. Wonderful. Out of this world.

MEG. I know. My father gave it to me. (*Placing drum on table.*) Doesn't it make a beautiful noise?

GOLDBERG. It's a fine piece of work. Maybe Stan'll play us a little tune afterwards.

MEG. Oh, yes. Will you, Stan?

STANLEY. Could I have my glasses?

GOLDBERG. Ah, yes. (*He holds his hand out to* Mc-CANN. McCANN *passes him his glasses.*) Here they are. (*He holds them out for* STANLEY, *who reaches for them.*) Here they are. (STANLEY *takes them.*) Now. What have we got here? (*To the sideboard.*) Enough to scuttle a liner. We've got four bottles of Scotch and one bottle of Irish.

MEG. Oh, Mr. Goldberg, what should I drink?

GOLDBERG. Glasses, glasses first. Open the Scotch, McCann.

MEG. (*Crosses to the kitchen.*) Here's my very best glasses in here.

McCANN. I don't drink Scotch.

GOLDBERG. You've got the Irish.

MEG. (*Bringing the glasses.*) Here they are.

GOLDBERG. Good, Mrs. Boles. I think Stanley should pour the toast, don't you?

MEG. Oh, yes. Come on, Stanley. (STANLEY *walks slowly to the table.*) Do you like my dress, Mr. Goldberg?

GOLDBERG. It's out on its own. Turn yourself round a minute. I used to be in the business. Go on, walk up there.

MEG. Oh, no.

GOLDBERG. Don't be shy. (*He slaps her bottom.*)

MEG. Oooh!

GOLDBERG. Walk up the boulevard. Let's have a look at you. (*She crosses Upstage.*) What a carriage. What's your opinion, McCann? Like a Countess, nothing less. Madam, now turn about and give us a little promenade. (*She walks* D. L. *and circles the armchair.*) What a deportment!

McCANN. (*To* STANLEY.) You can pour my Irish too.

GOLDBERG. You look like a gladiola.

MEG. Stan, what about my dress?

GOLDBERG. One for the lady, one for the lady. Now madam—your glass.

MEG. Thank you.

GOLDBERG. Lift your glasses, ladies and gentlemen. We'll drink a toast.

MEG. Lulu isn't here.

GOLDBERG. It's past the hour. Now—who's going to propose the toast? Mrs. Boles, it can only be you.

MEG. Me?

GOLDBERG. Who else?

MEG. But what do I say?

GOLDBERG. Say what you feel. What you honestly feel. (MEG *looks uncertain.*) It's Stanley's birthday. Your Stanley. Look at him. Look at him and it'll come. Wait a minute, the light's too strong. Let's have proper lighting. McCann, have you got your torch?

MCCANN. (*Bringing a small torch from his pocket.*) Here.

GOLDBERG. Switch out the light and put on your torch. (MCCANN *goes to the door,* U. C. *switches off the LIGHT, comes back, shines the torch on* MEG. *Outside the window there is still a faint LIGHT.*) Not on the lady, on the gentleman! You must shine it on the birthday boy. (MC-CANN *shines the torch in* STANLEY'S *face.* GOLDBERG *goes to the window seat.*) Now, Mrs. Boles, it's all yours.

(MEG *crosses to table* C. *Pause.*)

MEG. I don't know what to say.

GOLDBERG. Look at him. Just look at him.

MEG. Isn't the light in his eyes?

GOLDBERG. No, no. Go on.

MEG. Well—it's very, very nice to be here tonight, in my house, and I want to propose a toast to Stanley, because it's his birthday, and he's lived here for a long while now, and he's my Stanley now. And I think he's a good boy, although sometimes he's bad. (*An appreciative laugh from* GOLDBERG.) And he's the only Stanley I know, and I know him better than all the world, although he doesn't think so. (*"Hear— Hear" from* GOLDBERG.) Well, I could cry because I'm so happy, having him here and

not gone away, on his birthday, and there isn't anything
I wouldn't do for him, and all you good people here tonight . . . (*She sobs and sits above table.*)

GOLDBERG. Beautiful! A beautiful speech. Put the light
on, McCann. (MCCANN *goes to the door.* STANLEY *remains still.*) That was a lovely toast. (*The LIGHT goes
on.* LULU *enters from the door,* L. GOLDBERG *comforts*
MEG.) Buck up now. Come on, smile at the birdy. That's
better. We've got to drink yet. Ah, look who's here.

MEG. Lulu.

GOLDBERG. How do you do, Lulu? I'm Nat Goldberg.
(*He kisses her hand.*) Stanley, a drink for your guest.
You just missed the toast, my dear, and what a toast.

LULU. Did I?

GOLDBERG. Stanley, a drink for your guest. Stanley.
(STANLEY *hands a glass to* LULU.) Right. Now raise your
glasses. Everyone standing up? No? not you, Stanley.
You must sit down.

MCCANN. (U. C. *below stairs.*) Yes, that's right. He
must sit down.

GOLDBERG. You don't mind sitting down a minute?
We're going to drink to you.

MEG. (*Crosses to* STANLEY.) Come on! (STANLEY *sits
in a chair at* L. *of table.*)

GOLDBERG. Right. Now Stanley's sat down. (*Taking
the Stage.*) Well, I want to say first that I've never been
so touched to the heart as by the toast we've just heard.
How often, in this day and age, do you come across real,
true warmth? Once in a lifetime. Until a few minutes ago,
ladies and gentlemen, I, like all of you, was asking the
same question. What's happened to the love, the bon-
homie, the unashamed expression of affection of the day
before yesterday, that our mums taught us in the nursery?

MCCANN. Gone with the wind.

GOLDBERG. That's what I thought, until today. I believe in a good laugh, a day's fishing, a bit of gardening.
I was very proud of my old greenhouse, made out of my
own spit and faith. That's the sort of man I am. Not size

but quality. A little Austin, tea in Fullers, a library book from Boots, and I'm satisfied. But just now, I say just now, the lady of the house said her piece and I for one am knocked over by the sentiments she expressed. Lucky is the man who's at the receiving end, that's what I say. (*Pause.*) How can I put it to you? We all wander on our tod through this world. It's a lonely pillow to kip on. Right!

LULU. (*Admiringly.*) Right!

GOLDBERG. Agreed. But tonight, Lulu, McCann, we've known a great fortune. We've heard a lady extend the sum total of her devotion, in all its pride, plume and peacock, to a member of her own living race. Stanley, my heartfelt congratulations. I wish you, on behalf of us all, a happy birthday. I'm sure you've never been a prouder man than you are today. Mazoltov! And may we only meet at Simchahs! (LULU *and* MEG *applaud.*) Turn out the light, McCann, while we drink the toast.

LULU. That was a wonderful speech.

(McCANN *switches out the LIGHT, comes back, and shines the torch in* STANLEY'S *face. The LIGHT outside the window is fainter.*)

GOLDBERG. Lift your glasses. Stanley—happy birthday.

McCANN. Happy birthday.

LULU. Happy birthday.

MEG. Many happy returns of the day, Stan.

GOLDBERG. And well over the fast.

(*They all drink.*)

MEG. (*Kissing him.*) Oh, Stanny . . .

GOLDBERG. Lights!

McCANN. Right! (*He switches on the LIGHTS.*)

MEG. Clink my glass, Stan.

LULU. Mr. Goldberg—

GOLDBERG. Call me Nat.

MEG. (*To* McCANN *at sideboard.*) You clink my glass.

LULU. (*To* GOLDBERG.) You're empty. Let me fill you
up. (*Crosses to sideboard for bottle.*)

GOLDBERG. It's a pleasure. (*Watching her go.*)

LULU. You're a marvelous speaker, Nat, you know
that? Where did you learn to speak like that?

GOLDBERG. You liked it, eh? (*They cross to the armchair.*)

LULU. Oh, yes!

GOLDBERG. Well, my first chance to stand up and give
a lecture was at the Ethical Hall, Bayswater. A wonderful opportunity. I'll never forget it. They were all there
that night. Charlotte Street was empty. Of course, that's
a good while ago.

LULU. What did you speak about?

GOLDBERG. The Necessary and the Possible. It went like
a bomb. Since then I always speak at weddings.

(STANLEY *is still.* GOLDBERG *sits in the armchair.* MEG
joins McCANN D. R. LULU *is* D. L. McCANN *pours
more Irish from the bottle, which he carries, into his
glass.*)

MEG. Let's have some of yours.

McCANN. In that?

MEG. Yes.

McCANN. Are you used to mixing them?

MEG. No.

McCANN. Give me your glass.

(MEG *sits* R. *of table.* LULU *pours more drink for* GOLD-
BERG *and herself, and gives* GOLDBERG *his glass.*)

GOLDBERG. Thank you.

MEG. (*To* McCANN.) Do you think I should?

GOLDBERG. Lulu, you're a big bouncy girl. Come and sit
on my lap.

McCANN. Why not?

LULU. Do you think I should?

GOLDBERG. Try it.

MEG. (*Sipping.*) Very nice.

LULU. I'll bounce up to the ceiling.

McCANN. I don't know how you can mix that stuff.

GOLDBERG. Take a chance.

(LULU *sits on* GOLDBERG's *lap.*)

MEG. (*To* McCANN.) Sit down on this stool.

McCANN. This?

GOLDBERG. Comfortable?

LULU. Yes, thanks.

McCANN. (*Sitting.*) It's comfortable.

GOLDBERG. You know, there's a lot in your eyes.

LULU. And in yours, too.

GOLDBERG. Do you think so?

LULU. (*Giggling.*) Go on!

McCANN. (*To* MEG.) Where'd you get it?

MEG. My father gave it to me.

LULU. I didn't know I was going to meet you here to-night.

McCANN. (*To* MEG.) Ever been to Carrikmacross?

MEG. (*Drinking.*) I've been to King's Cross.

LULU. You came right out the blue, you know that?

GOLDBERG. (*As she moves.*) Mind how you go. You're cracking a rib.

MEG. (*Standing.*) I want to dance! (LULU *and* GOLD-ßERG *look into each other's eyes.* McCANN *drinks.* MEG *crosses to* STANLEY.) Stanley. Dance.

(STANLEY *sits still.* MEG *dances round the room alone, then comes back to* McCANN, *who fills her glass. She sits on the stool with* McCANN.)

LULU. (*To* GOLDBERG.) Shall I tell you something?

GOLDBERG. What?

LULU. I trust you.

GOLDBERG. (*Lifting his glass.*) Gesundheit.

LULU. Have you got a wife?

GOLDBERG. I had a wife. What a wife. Listen to this,
Friday, of an afternoon, I'd take myself for a little constitutional, down over the park. Eh, do me a favour, just
sit up here a minute, will you? (LULU *sits on the arm.
He stretches and continues, crossing to the window seat
and above the chair to the table* C.) A little constitutional.
I'd say hullo to the little boys, the little girls—I never
made distinctions—and then back I'd go, back to my
bungalow with the flat roof. "Simey," my wife used to
shout, "quick, before it gets cold!" And there on the
table what would I see? The nicest piece of rollmop and
pickled cucumber you could wish to find on a plate.

LULU. I thought your name was Nat.

GOLDBERG. She called me Simey.

LULU. I bet you were a good husband.

GOLDBERG. You should have seen her funeral.

LULU. Why?

GOLDBERG. (*Draws in his breath and wags his head.*)
What a funeral. (*Crosses back to* LULU.)

MEG. (*To* MCCANN.) My father was going to take me
to Ireland once. But then he went away by himself.

LULU. (*To* GOLDBERG.) Do you think you knew me
when I was a little girl?

GOLDBERG. Were you a nice little girl?

LULU. I was.

MEG. I don't know if he went to Ireland.

GOLDBERG. Maybe I played piggy-back with you.

LULU. Maybe you did.

MEG. He didn't take me.

GOLDBERG. (*Sitting in chair with* LULU.) Or pop goes
the weasel.

LULU. Is that a game?

GOLDBERG. Sure it's a game!

MCCANN. Why didn't he take you to Ireland?

LULU. You're tickling me!

GOLDBERG. You should worry.

LULU. I've always liked older men. They can soothe you.

(*They embrace.*)

MCCANN. I know a place. Roscrea. Mother Nolan's.

MEG. There was a night-light in my room, when I was a little girl.

MCCANN. One time I stayed there all night with the boys. Singing and drinking all night.

MEG. And my Nanny used to sit up with me, and sing songs to me.

MCCANN. And a plate of fry in the morning. Now where am I?

MEG. My little room was pink. I had a pink carpet and pink curtains, and I had musical boxes all over the room. And they played me to sleep. And my father was a very big doctor. That's why I never had any complaints. I was cared for, and I had little sisters and brothers in other rooms, all different colours.

MCCANN. Tullamore, where are you?

MEG. (*To* MCCANN.) Give us a drop more.

MCCANN. (*Filling her glass and singing.*) Glorio, Glorio, to the bold Fenian men!

MEG. Oh, what a lovely voice.

GOLDBERG. Give us a song, McCann.

LULU. A love song!

MCCANN. (*Crosses to above table and puts his hand on* STANLEY'S *shoulder. Reciting.*) The night that poor Paddy was stretched, the boys they all paid him a visit.

GOLDBERG. A love song!

MCCANN. (*In a full voice, sings.*)
Oh, the Garden of Eden has vanished, they say,
But I know the lie of it still.
Just turn to the left at the foot of Ben Clay
And stop when halfway to Coote Hill.
It's there you will find it, I know sure enough,
And its whispering over to me:

Come back, Paddy Reilly, to Bally-James-Duff,
Come home, Paddy Reilly, to me!
    (*He sits* L. *of table.*)

LULU. (*On* GOLDBERG'S *lap. To* GOLDBERG.) You're the dead image of the first man I ever loved.

GOLDBERG. It goes without saying.

MEG. (*Reaches to put drink on table and slides off stool to the floor.*) I want to play a game!

GOLDBERG. A game?

LULU. What game?

MEG. Any game.

LULU. (*Jumping up.*) Yes, let's play a game.

GOLDBERG. What game?

McCANN. Hide and seek.

LULU. Blind man's buff.

MEG. Yes.

GOLDBERG. You want to play blind man's buff?

LULU and MEG. Yes!

GOLDBERG. All right. Blind man's buff. Come on! Everyone up! (*Rising.*) McCann. Stanley—Stanley!

MEG. Stanley. Up.

GOLDBERG. What's the matter with him?

MEG. (*Bending over him.*) Stanley, we're going to play a game. Oh, come on, don't be sulky, Stan.

(STANLEY *rises.* McCANN *rises.*)

GOLDBERG. Right! Now—who's going to be blind first?

LULU. Mrs. Boles.

MEG. Not me.

GOLDBERG. Of course you.

MEG. Who, me?

LULU. (*Taking her scarf from her neck.*) Here you are.

McCANN. How do you play this game?

LULU. (*Tying her scarf round* MEG'S *eyes.*) Haven't you ever played blind man's buff? Keep still, Mrs. Boles. You mustn't be touched. But you can't move after she's blind. You must stay where you are after she's blind. And

if she touches you then you become blind. Turn round.
How many fingers am I holding up?

MEG. I can't see.

LULU. Right.

GOLDBERG. Right! Everyone move about. McCann.
Stanley. Now stop. Now still. Off you go!

(STANLEY *is* D. R., MEG *moves about the room.* GOLDBERG
fondles LULU *behind armchair.* MEG *touches* Mc-
CANN.)

MEG. Caught you!

LULU. Take off your scarf.

MEG. What lovely hair!

LULU. (*Untying the scarf.*) There.

MEG. It's you!

GOLDBERG. Put it on, McCann.

LULU. (*Tying it on* MCCANN.) There. Turn round.
How many fingers am I holding up?

MCCANN. I don't know.

GOLDBERG. Right! Everyone move about. Right. Stop!
Still!

(LULU *and* GOLDBERG *are on the stairs.* MCCANN *begins
to move.* STANLEY *is at the sideboard.*)

MEG. (*Circling the table.*) Oh, this is lovely!

GOLDBERG. Quiet! Tch, tch, tch. Now—all move again.
(MEG *to armchair.*) Stop! Still!

(MCCANN *moves about.* GOLDBERG, U. C., *fondles* LULU *at
arm's length.* MCCANN *draws near* STANLEY. *He
stretches his arm and touches* STANLEY'S *glasses.*)

MEG. It's Stanley!

GOLDBERG. (*To* LULU.) Enjoying the game?

MEG. It's your turn, Stan.

McCANN. (*He takes off the scarf. To* STANLEY.) I'll take your glasses. (McCANN *takes* STANLEY'S *glasses.*)

MEG. Give me the scarf.

GOLDBERG. (*Holding* LULU.) Tie his scarf, Mrs. Boles.

MEG. That's what I'm doing. (*She stands on the stool. To* STANLEY.) Can you see my nose?

GOLDBERG. He can't. Ready? Right! Everyone move. Stop! And still!

(STANLEY *stands blindfold.* McCANN *backs slowly across the Stage to* L. *He breaks* STANLEY'S *glasses, snapping the frames.* MEG *is* D. L., LULU *and* GOLDBERG U. C., *close together.* STANLEY *begins to move, very slowly, across the Stage to* L. McCANN *picks up the drum and places it sideways in* STANLEY'S *path.* STANLEY *walks into the drum and falls over with his foot caught in it.*)

MEG. Ooh!

GOLDBERG. Sssh!

(STANLEY *rises. He begins to move towards* MEG, *dragging the drum on his foot. He reaches her and stops. His hands move towards her and they reach her throat. He begins to strangle her.* McCANN *and* GOLDBERG *rush forward and throw him off. BLACKOUT. There is now no light at all through the window. The Stage is in darkness.*)

LULU. The lights!

GOLDBERG. What's happened?

LULU. The lights!

McCANN. Wait a minute.

GOLDBERG. Where is he?

McCANN. Let go of me!

GOLDBERG. Who's this?

LULU. Someone's touching me!

McCANN. Where is he?

MEG. Why has the light gone out!

GOLDBERG. Where's your torch? (McCANN *shines the torch in* GOLDBERG'S *face,* U. C.) Not on me!

McCANN. (*He shifts the torch. It is knocked down from from his hand and falls. It goes out.*) My torch!

LULU. Oh, God!

GOLDBERG. Where's your torch? Pick up your torch!

McCANN. I can't find it.

LULU. Hold me. Hold me.

GOLDBERG. Get down on your knees. Help him find the torch.

LULU. I can't.

McCANN. It's gone.

MEG. Why has the light gone out?

GOLDBERG. Everyone quiet! Help him find the torch.

(*Silence. Grunts from* McCANN *and* GOLDBERG *on their knees. Suddenly there is a sharp, sustained rat-a-tat with a stick on the side of the drum from the back of the room. Silence. Whimpers from* LULU.)

GOLDBERG. Over here, McCann!

McCANN. Here.

GOLDBERG. Come to me, come to me. Easy. Over there.

(GOLDBERG *and* McCANN *move* U. L. *of the table.* STANLEY *moves* D. R. *of the table.* LULU *suddenly perceives him moving towards her, screams and faints.* GOLDBERG *and* McCANN *turn and stumble against each other.*) What is it?

McCANN. Who's that?

GOLDBERG. What is it?

(*In the darkness* STANLEY *picks up* LULU *and places her on the table.*)

MEG. It's Lulu!

(GOLDBERG *and* McCANN *move* D. R.)

GOLDBERG. Where is she?

MCCANN. She fell.

GOLDBERG. Where?

MCCANN. About here.

GOLDBERG. Help me pick her up.

MCCANN. (*Moving* D. L.) I can't find her.

GOLDBERG. She must be somewhere.

MCCANN. She's not here.

GOLDBERG. (*Moving* U. R.) She must be.

MCCANN. She's gone.

(MCCANN *finds the torch on the floor, shines it on the table and* STANLEY. LULU *is lying spread-eagled on the table,* STANLEY *bent over her.* STANLEY, *as soon as the torchlight hits him, begins to giggle.* GOLDBERG *and* MCCANN *move towards him. He backs, giggling, the torch on his face. They follow him Upstage. He backs against the sideboard, giggling. The torch draws closer. His giggle rises and grows as he flattens himself against the wall. Their figures converge upon him.*)

CURTAIN

ACT THREE

The next morning. PETEY *enters,* L., *with a newspaper, hangs up pouch and ticket machine as before, and sits at the table. He begins to read.* MEG'S *voice comes through the kitchen hatch.*

MEG. Is that you, Stan? (*Pause.*) Stanny?

PETEY. Yes?

MEG. Is that you?

PETEY. It's me.

MEG. (*Appearing at the hatch.*) Oh, it's you. I've run out of cornflakes.

PETEY. Well, what else have you got?

MEG. Nothing.

PETEY. Nothing?

MEG. Just a minute. (*She leaves the hatch and enters by the kitchen door.*) You got your paper?

PETEY. Yes.

MEG. Is it good?

PETEY. Not bad.

MEG. The two gentlemen had the last of the fry this morning.

PETEY. Oh, did they?

MEG. There's some tea in the pot, though. (*She pours tea for him.*) I'm going out shopping in a minute. Get you something nice. I've got a splitting headache.

PETEY. (*Reading.*) You slept like a log last night.

MEG. Did I?

PETEY. Dead out.

MEG. I must have been tired. (*She looks about the room and sees the broken drum under the sideboard.*) Oh, look. (*She rises and picks it up.*) The drum's broken. (PETEY *looks up.*) Why is it broken?

PETEY. I don't know.

62

(*She hits it with her hand.*)

MEG. It still makes a noise.

PETEY. You can always get another one.

MEG. (*Sadly.*) It was probably broken in the party. I don't remember it being broken, though, in the party. (*She puts it down on the sideboard.*) What a shame.

PETEY. You can always get another one, Meg.

MEG. Well, at least he did have it on his birthday, didn't he? Like I wanted him to.

PETEY. (*Reading.*) Yes.

MEG. Have you seen him down yet? (PETEY *does not answer.*) Petey.

PETEY. What?

MEG. Have you seen him down?

PETEY. Who?

MEG. Stanley.

PETEY. No.

MEG. Nor have I. That boy should be up. He's late for his breakfast.

PETEY. There isn't any breakfast.

MEG. Yes, but he doesn't know that. (*Crosses to stairs*). I'm going to call him.

PETEY. (*Quickly.*) No, don't do that, Meg. Let him sleep.

MEG. But you say he stays in bed too much.

PETEY. Let him sleep . . . this morning. Leave him.

MEG. (*Crossing back to* R. *of table.*) I've been up once, with his cup of tea. But Mr. McCann opened the door. He said they were talking. He said he'd made him one. He must have been up early. I don't know what they were talking about. I was surprised. Because Stanley's usually fast asleep when I wake him. But he wasn't this morning. I heard him talking. (*Pause.*) Do you think they know each other? I think they're old friends. Stanley had a lot of friends. I know he did. (*Pause.*) I didn't give him his tea. He'd already had one. I came down again and went on with my work. Then, after a bit, they came down to breakfast. Stanley must have gone to sleep again.

(*Pause.*)

PETEY. When are you going to do your shopping, Meg?

MEG. (*Crosses* U. C. *for hat and coat.*) Yes, I must. I've got a rotten headache. (*She goes to the window,* L., *stops suddenly and turns.*) Did you see what's outside this morning?

PETEY. What?

MEG. That big car.

PETEY. Yes.

MEG. It wasn't there yesterday. Did you . . . did you have a look inside it?

PETEY. I had a peep.

MEG. (*Coming down tensely, and whispering.*) Is there anything in it?

PETEY. In it?

MEG. Yes.

PETEY. What do you mean, in it?

MEG. Inside it.

PETEY. What sort of thing?

MEG. Well . . . I mean . . . is there . . . is there a wheelbarrow in it?

PETEY. A wheelbarrow?

MEG. Yes.

PETEY. I didn't see one.

MEG. You didn't. Are you sure?

PETEY. What would Mr. Goldberg want with a wheelbarrow?

MEG. Mr. Goldberg?

PETEY. It's his car.

MEG. (*Relieved.*) His car? Oh, I didn't know it was his car.

PETEY. Of course it's his car.

MEG. (*Sits in the armchair.*) Oh, I feel better.

PETEY. What are you on about?

MEG. Oh, I do feel better.

PETEY. You go and get a bit of air.

MEG. Yes, I will. I'll go and get the shopping. (*She goes towards the back door. A DOOR slams upstairs. She turns.*) It's Stanley! He's coming down—what am I going to do about his breakfast? (*She rushes into the kitchen.*) Petey, what shall I give him? (*She looks through the hatch.*) There's no cornflakes.

(*They* BOTH *gaze at the stairs. Enter* GOLDBERG. *He halts on the landing, as he meets their gaze, then smiles.*)

GOLDBERG. A reception committee!

MEG. Oh, I thought it was Stanley.

GOLDBERG. You find a resemblance?

MEG. Oh, no. You look quite different.

GOLDBERG. (*Coming into the room. Hangs hat and briefcase* U. C.) Different build, of course.

MEG. I thought he was coming down for his breakfast. He hasn't had his breakfast yet.

GOLDBERG. (*Crosses to table and pours tea.*) Your wife makes a very nice cup of tea, Mr. Boles, you know that?

PETEY. Yes, she does sometimes. Sometimes she forgets.

MEG. Is he coming down?

GOLDBERG. Down? Of course he's coming down. On a lovely sunny day like this he shouldn't come down? He'll be up and about in next to no time. (*He sits above the table.*) And what a breakfast he's going to get.

MEG. (L. C.) Mr. Goldberg.

GOLDBERG. Yes?

MEG. I didn't know that was your car outside.

GOLDBERG. You like it?

MEG. (*Crossing in.*) Are you going to go for a ride?

GOLDBERG. (*To* PETEY.) A smart car, eh?

PETEY. Nice shine on it, all right.

GOLDBERG. What is old is good, take my tip. There's room there. Room in the front, and room in the back. (*He strokes the teapot.*) The pot's hot. More tea, Mr. Boles?

PETEY. No, thanks.

MEG. Are you going to go for a ride?

GOLDBERG. (*Ruminatively.*) And the boot. A beautiful boot. There's just room . . . for the right amount.

MEG. Well, I'd better be off now. (*She moves to the* U. C. *door, and turns.*) Petey, when Stanley comes down . . .

PETEY. Yes?

MEG. Tell him I won't be long.

PETEY. I'll tell him.

MEG. (*Vaguely.*) I won't be long. (*She exits.*)

GOLDBERG. (*Sipping his tea.*) A good woman. A charming woman. My mother was the same. My wife was identical.

PETEY. How is he this morning?

GOLDBERG. Who?

PETEY. Stanley. Is he any better?

GOLDBERG. (*A little uncertainly.*) Oh . . . a little better, I think, a little better. Of course. I'm not really qualified to say, Mr. Boles. I mean, I haven't got the . . . the qualifications. The best thing would be if someone with the proper . . . mnn . . . qualifications . . . was to have a look at him. Someone with a few letters after his name. It makes all the difference.

PETEY. Yes.

GOLDBERG. (*Rises to French doors* R.) Anyway, Dermot's with him at the moment. He's . . . keeping him company.

PETEY. Dermot?

GOLDBERG. Yes.

PETEY. It's a terrible thing.

GOLDBERG. (*Sighs.*) Yes. The birthday celebration was too much for him.

PETEY. What came over him?

GOLDBERG. (*Sharply.*) What came over him? Breakdown, Mr. Boles. Pure and simple. Nervous breakdown.

PETEY. But what brought it on so suddenly?

GOLDBERG. (*Crossing in to* R. *of table.*) Well, Mr. Boles, it can happen in all sorts of ways. A friend of mine was telling me about it only the other day. We'd both been concerned with another case—not entirely similar, of course, but . . . quite alike, quite alike. (*He pauses. Crosses to window seat.*) Anyway, he was telling me, you see, this friend of mine, that sometimes it happens gradual—day by day it grows and grows and grows . . . day by day. And then other times it happens all at once. Poof! Like that! The nerves break. There's no guarantee how it's going to happen, but with certain people . . . it's a foregone conclusion.

PETEY. Really?

GOLDBERG. Yes. This friend of mine—he was telling me about it—only the other day. (*He stands uneasily for a moment, then brings out a cigarette case and takes a cigarette.*) Have an Abdullah.

PETEY. No, no, I don't take them.

GOLDBERG. Once in a while I treat myself to a cigarette. An Abdullah, perhaps, or a . . . (*He snaps his fingers.*)

PETEY. What a night. (GOLDBERG *lights his cigarette with a lighter.* PETEY *puts cups, plates, etc., on tray.*) Came in the front door and all the lights were out. Put a shilling in the slot, came in here and the party was over.

GOLDBERG. (*Coming Downstage.*) You put a shilling in the slot?

PETEY. Yes.

GOLDBERG. (*With a short laugh.*) I could have sworn it was a fuse.

PETEY. (*Puts tray on hatch shelf and crosses* L. *to* GOLDBERG, *continuing.*) There was dead silence. Couldn't hear a thing. So I went upstairs and your friend—Dermot—met me on the landing. And he told me.

GOLDBERG. (*Sharply.*) Who?

PETEY. Your friend—Dermot.

GOLDBERG. (*Heavily.*) Dermot. Yes. (*He sits in the armchair.*)

PETEY. They get over it sometimes though, don't they? I mean, they can recover from it, can't they?

GOLDBERG. Recover? Yes, sometimes they recover, in one way or another.

PETEY. I mean, he might have recovered by now, mightn't he?

GOLDBERG. It's conceivable. Conceivable.

PETEY. (*He starts to the kitchen.*) Well, if he's no better by lunchtime I'll go and get hold of a doctor.

GOLDBERG. (*Briskly.*) It's all taken care of, Mr. Boles. Don't worry yourself.

PETEY. (*Dubiously.*) What do you mean? (*A DOOR slams upstairs. They look towards the door. Enter Mc-CANN with two suitcases.*) Oh, it's you. All packed up?

(PETEY *takes the teapot and cups into the kitchen. Mc-CANN crosses L. and puts down the suitcases. He goes up to the window and looks out.*)

GOLDBERG. Well? (MCCANN *does not answer.*) McCann. I asked you "well."

MCCANN. (*Without turning.*) Well what?

GOLDBERG. What's what? (MCCANN *does not answer.*) What is what?

MCCANN. (*Turning to look at* GOLDBERG, *grimly.*) I'm not going up there again.

GOLDBERG. Why not?

MCCANN. I'm not going up there again.

GOLDBERG. What's going on now?

MCCANN. (*Moving down.*) He's quiet now. He stopped all that . . . talking a while ago.

(PETEY *appears at the kitchen hatch, unnoticed.*)

GOLDBERG. When will he be ready?

MCCANN. (*Sullenly.*) You can go up yourself next time.

GOLDBERG. What's the matter with you?

MCCANN. (*Quietly.*) I gave him . . .

GOLDBERG. What?

MCCANN. I gave him his glasses.

GOLDBERG. Wasn't he glad to get them back?

McCANN. The frames are bust.

GOLDBERG. How did that happen?

McCANN. He tried to fit the eyeholes into his eyes. I left him doing it.

PETEY. (*Enters from the kitchen and goes to the side-board.*) There's some Sellotape somewhere. We can stick them together.

(GOLDBERG *and* McCANN *turn to see him. Pause.*)

GOLDBERG. (*Rises to* U. C.) Sellotape? No, no, that's all right, Mr. Boles. It'll keep him quiet for the time being, keep his mind off other things.

PETEY. (*Moving to* GOLDBERG.) What about a doctor?

GOLDBERG. It's all taken care of.

(McCANN *moves over* L. *to the shoe-box below window seat, and takes out a brush and brushes his shoes.*)

PETEY. (*Moves to the table.*) I think he needs one.

GOLDBERG. I agree with you. It's all taken care of. We'll give him a bit of time to settle down, and then I'll take him to Monty.

PETEY. You're going to take him to a doctor?

GOLDBERG. (*Staring at him.*) Sure, Monty. (*Pause.* McCANN *brushes his shoes.* PETEY *folds the tablecloth and puts it in the sideboard.* GOLDBERG *sits* L. *of table.*) So Mrs. Boles has gone out to get us something nice for lunch?

PETEY. That's right.

GOLDBERG. Unfortunately we may be gone by then.

PETEY. Will you?

GOLDBERG. By then we may be gone.

(*Pause.*)

PETEY. Well, I think I'll see how my peas are getting on, in the meantime.

GOLDBERG. The meantime?

PETEY. While we're waiting.

GOLDBERG. Waiting for what? (PETEY *walks towards the French doors.*) Aren't you going back to the beach?

PETEY. No, not yet. Give me a call when he comes down, will you, Mr. Goldberg?

GOLDBERG. (*Rises to* U. C. *Earnestly.*) You'll have a crowded beach today . . . on a day like this. They'll be lying on their backs, swimming out to sea. My life. What about the deck-chairs? Are the deck-chairs ready?

PETEY. I put them all out this morning.

GOLDBERG. (*Offering the ticket machine.*) But what about the tickets? Who's going to take the tickets?

PETEY. (*Ignoring it.*) That's all right. That'll be all right, Mr. Goldberg. Don't worry about that. I'll be back.

(*He exits* R. GOLDBERG *puts down the machine, crosses* R. *and looks after him.* MCCANN *crosses to the table, sits, picks up the paper and begins to tear it into strips.*)

GOLDBERG. (*At French doors.*) Is everything ready?

MCCANN. (R. *of table.*) Sure.

(GOLDBERG *walks heavily, brooding, to the table. He sits* L. *of it noticing what* MCCANN *is doing.*)

GOLDBERG. Stop doing that!

MCCANN. What?

GOLDBERG. Why do you do that all the time? It's childish, it's pointless. It's without a solitary point.

MCCANN. What's the matter with you today?

GOLDBERG. Questions, questions. Stop asking me so many questions. What do you think I am?

MCCANN. (*He studies him. He then folds the paper,*

leaving the strips inside.) Well? (*Pause.* GOLDBERG *leans
back in the chair, his eyes closed.*) Well?

GOLDBERG. (*With fatigue.*) Well what?

MCCANN. Do we wait or do we go and get him?

GOLDBERG. (*Slowly.*) You want to go and get him?

MCCANN. I want to get it over.

GOLDBERG. That's understandable.

MCCANN. So do we wait or do we—?

GOLDBERG. (*Interrupting.*) I don't know why, but I feel
knocked out. I feel a bit . . . It's uncommon for me.

MCCANN. Is that so?

GOLDBERG. It's unusual.

MCCANN. (*Rising swiftly and going behind* GOLDBERG'S
chair. Hissing.) Let's finish and go. Let's get it over and
go. Get the thing done. Let's finish the bloody thing. Let's
get the thing done and go! (*Pause.*) Will I go up?
(*Pause.*) Nat! (GOLDBERG *sits humped.* MCCANN *slips to
his* L. *side.*) Simey!

GOLDBERG. (*Opening his eyes, regarding* MCCANN.)
What—did—you—call—me?

MCCANN. Who?

GOLDBERG. (*Murderously.*) Don't call me that! (*He
seizes* MCCANN *by the throat and throws him to the
floor.*) NEVER CALL ME THAT!

MCCANN. (*Writhing.*) Nat, Nat, Nat, NAT! I called
you Nat. I was asking you, Nat. Honest to God. Just a
question, that's all, just a question, do you see, do you
follow me?

GOLDBERG. What question?

MCCANN. Will I go up?

GOLDBERG. (*Violently.*) Up? I thought you weren't
going to go up there again?

MCCANN. What do you mean? Why not!

GOLDBERG. You said so!

MCCANN. I never said that!

GOLDBERG. No?

MCCANN. (*From the floor, to the room at large.*) Who

said that? I never said that! I'll go up now! (*He jumps up and rushes to the stairs.*)

GOLDBERG Wait! (*He stretches his arms to the arms of the chair.*) Come here. (MCCANN *approaches him very slowly.*) I want your opinion. Have a look in my mouth. (*He opens his mouth wide.*) Take a good look. (MCCANN *looks.*) You know what I mean? (MCCANN *peers.*) You know what? I've never lost a tooth. Not since the day I was born. Nothing's changed. (*He gets up, crosses* L.) That's why I've reached my position, McCann. Because I've always been as fit as a fiddle. All my life I've said the same. Play up, play up, and play the game. Honour thy father and thy Mother. All along the line. Follow the line, the line, McCann, and you can't go wrong. What do you think, I'm a self-made man? No! I sat where I was told to sit. I kept my eye on the ball. School? Don't talk to me about school. Top in all subjects. And for why? Because I'm telling you, I'm telling you, follow my line? Follow my mental? Learn by heart. Never write down a thing. No. And don't go too near the water. And you'll find—that what I say is true. Because I believe that the world . . . (*Vacant.*) . . . Because I believe that the world . . . (*Desperate.*) . . . BECAUSE I BELIEVE THAT THE WORLD . . . (*Lost. He sits in armchair.*) Sit down, McCann, sit here where I can look at you. (MCCANN *sits on the footstool. Intensely, with growing certainty.*) My father said to me, Benny, Benny, he said, come here. He was dying. I knelt down. By him day and night. Who else was there? Forgive, Benny, he said, and let live. Yes, Dad. Go home to your wife. I will, Dad. Keep an eye open for low-lives, for schnorrers and for layabouts. He didn't mention names. I lost my life in the service of others, he said, I'm not ashamed. Do your duty and keep your observations. Always bid good morning to the neighbours. Never, never forget your family, for they are the rock, the constitution and the core! If you're ever in any difficulties Uncle Barney will see you in the clear. I knelt down. (*He kneels facing* MCCANN.) I swore on the good book. And I knew the word I had to remember— Respect! Because McCann— (*Gently.*) Seamus— who came before your father? His father. And who came before him? Before him? . . . (*Vacant—triumphant.*) Who came before your father's father but your father's father's mother! Your great-gran-granny. (*Silence. He slowly rises.*) And that's why I've reached my position, McCann. Because I've always been as fit as a fiddle. My motto. Work hard and play hard. Not a day's illness. (*He looks round. He sits in the armchair. Stopping.*) All the same, give me a blow. (*Pause.*) Blow in my mouth. (McCANN *stands, puts his hands on his knees, bends and blows in* GOLDBERG'S *mouth.*) One for the road.

(McCANN *blows again in his mouth.* GOLDBERG *breathes deeply, shakes his head.* LULU *enters from upstairs. Pause.*)

McCANN. (*At the foot of the stairs.*) I'll give you five minutes. (*He exits.*)

GOLDBERG. Come over here.

LULU. No, thank you.

GOLDBERG. What's the matter? You got the needle to Uncle Natey?

LULU. I'm going.

GOLDBERG. Have a game of pontoon first, for old time's sake.

LULU. I've had enough games.

GOLDBERG. A girl like you, at your age, at your time of health, and you don't take to games?

LULU. You're very smart.

GOLDBERG. Anyway, who says you don't take to them?

LULU. Do you think I'm like all the other girls?

GOLDBERG. Are all the other girls like that, too?

LULU. I don't know about any other girls.

GOLDBERG. Nor me. I've never touched another woman.

LULU. (*Distressed.*) What would my father say, if he knew? And what would Eddie say?

GOLDBERG. Eddie?

LULU. He was my first love, Eddie was. And whatever happened, it was pure. With him! He didn't come into my room at night with a briefcase!

GOLDBERG. Who opened the briefcase, me or you? Lulu, Schmulu, let bygones be bygones, do me a turn. (*Rises.*) Kiss and make up.

LULU. (*Crosses away below table to* R.) I wouldn't touch you.

GOLDBERG. (*To* L. *of table above.*) And today I'm leaving.

LULU. You're leaving?

GOLDBERG. Today.

LULU. (*Crosses to him. With growing anger.*) You used me for a night. A passing fancy.

GOLDBERG. Who used who?

LULU. You made use of me by cunning when my defences were down.

GOLDBERG. Who took them down?

LULU. That's what you did. You quenched your ugly thirst. You took advantage of me when I was overwrought. I wouldn't do those things again, not even for a Sultan!

GOLDBERG. One night doesn't make a harem.

LULU. You taught me things a girl shouldn't know before she's been married at least three times!

GOLDBERG. Now you're a jump ahead! What are you complaining about?

(*Enter* McCANN *quickly.*)

LULU. You didn't appreciate me for myself. You took all those liberties only to satisfy your appetite.

GOLDBERG. You wanted me to do it, Lulula, so I did it. (*Sits on the arm of the armchair.*)

McCANN. That's fair enough. (*Advancing.*) You had a long sleep, Miss.

LULU. (*Backing* L.) Me?

McCann. Your sort, you spend too much time in bed.

Lulu. What do you mean?

McCann. (*Following.*) Have you got anything to confess?

Lulu. What?

McCann. (*Savagely.*) Confess!

Lulu. (*Circles below table to* c.) Confess what?

McCann. Down on your knees and confess.

Lulu. What does he mean?

Goldberg. Confess. What can you lose?

Lulu. What, to him?

Goldberg. He's only been unfrocked six months.

McCann. (r. *of table.*) Kneel down, woman, and tell me the latest!

Lulu. (*Retreating to the* u. c. *door.*) I've seen every-thing that's happened. I know what's going on. I've a pretty shrewd idea.

McCann. (*Advancing.*) I've seen you hanging about the Rock of Cashel, profaning the soil with your goings-on. Out of my sight!

Lulu. I'm going.

(*She exits.* McCann *goes upstairs.* Goldberg *looks out French doors, sees drum on sideboard and gives it a few taps.* Stanley *enters, dressed in striped trousers, black jacket, and white collar. He carries a bowler hat in one hand and his broken glasses in the other. He is clean shaven.* McCann *follows.* Goldberg *meets* Stanley, *seats him in the armchair and puts his hat on the chair* l. *of table.*)

Goldberg. How are you, Stan? (*Pause.*) Are you feeling any better? (*Pause.*) What's happened to your glasses? (Goldberg *bends to look.*) They're broken. What a pity. (Stanley *stares blankly at the floor.*)

McCann. (*At the table.*) He looks better, doesn't he?

Goldberg. Much better.

McCann. A new man.

GOLDBERG. You know what we'll do?

McCANN. What?

GOLDBERG. We'll buy him another pair.

(*They begin to woo him, gently and with relish. During the following sequence* STANLEY *shows no reaction. He remains, with no movement, where he sits.*)

McCANN. Out of our pockets.

GOLDBERG. (*Crosses to* R. *of* STANLEY.) It goes without saying. Between you and me, Stan, it's about time you had a new pair of glasses.

McCANN. You can't see straight.

GOLDBERG. It's true. You've been cockeyed for years.

McCANN. Now you're even more cockeyed.

GOLDBERG. He's right. You've gone from bad to worse.

McCANN. Worse than worse.

GOLDBERG. You need a long convalescence.

McCANN. A change of air.

GOLDBERG. Somewhere over the rainbow.

McCANN. Where angels fear to tread.

GOLDBERG. Exactly.

McCANN. (*Moves to* L. *of* STANLEY.) You're in a rut.

GOLDBERG. You look anaemic.

McCANN. Rheumatic.

GOLDBERG. Myoptic.

McCANN. Epileptic.

GOLDBERG. You're on the verge.

McCANN. You're a dead duck.

GOLDBERG. But we can save you.

McCANN. From a worse fate.

GOLDBERG. True.

McCANN. Undeniable.

GOLDBERG. From now on, we'll be the hub of your wheel.

McCANN. We'll renew your season ticket.

GOLDBERG. We'll take tuppence off your morning tea.

McCANN. We'll give you a discount on all inflammable goods.

GOLDBERG. We'll watch over you.

McCANN. Advise you.

GOLDBERG. Give you proper care and treatment.

McCANN. Let you use the club bar.

GOLDBERG. Keep a table reserved.

McCANN. Help you acknowledge fast days.

GOLDBERG. Bake you cakes.

McCANN. Help you kneel on kneeling days.

GOLDBERG. Give you a free pass.

McCANN. Take you for constitutionals.

GOLDBERG. Give you hot tips.

McCANN. We'll provide the skipping rope.

GOLDBERG. The vest and pants.

McCANN. The ointment.

GOLDBERG. The hot poultice.

McCANN. The fingerstall.

GOLDBERG. The abdomen belt.

McCANN. The ear plugs.

GOLDBERG. The baby powder.

McCANN. The back scratcher.

GOLDBERG. The spare tyre.

McCANN. The stomach pump.

GOLDBERG. The oxygen tent.

McCANN. The prayer wheel.

GOLDBERG. The plaster of Paris.

McCANN. The crash helmet.

GOLDBERG. The crutches.

McCANN. A day and night service.

GOLDBERG. All on the house.

McCANN. That's it.

(They change places.)

GOLDBERG. We'll make a man of you.

McCANN. And a woman.

GOLDBERG. You'll be re-orientated.

McCANN. You'll be rich.

GOLDBERG. You'll be adjusted.

McCANN. You'll be our pride and joy.

GOLDBERG. You'll be a mensch.

McCANN. You'll be a success.

GOLDBERG. You'll be integrated.

McCANN. You'll give orders.

GOLDBERG. You'll make decisions.

McCANN. You'll be a magnate.

GOLDBERG. A statesman.

McCANN. You'll own yachts.

GOLDBERG. Animals.

McCANN. Animals.

GOLDBERG. (*He looks at* McCANN.) I said animals. (*He turns back to* STANLEY.) You'll be able to make or break, Stan. By my life. (*Silence.* STANLEY *is still.*) Well? What do you say? (STANLEY'S *head lifts very slowly and turns in* GOLDBERG'S *direction.*) What do you think? Eh, boy? (STANLEY *puts on the glasses, one in each eye.*)

McCANN. What's your opinion, sir? Of this prospect, sir?

GOLDBERG. Prospect. Sure. Sure it's a prospect. What's your opinion of such a prospect? Eh, Stanley.

(STANLEY *concentrates, his mouth opens, he attempts to speak, fails and emits sounds from his throat.*)

STANLEY. Uh-gug . . . uh-gug . . . eeehhh-gag . . . (*On the breath.*) Cahh . . . caahh . . .

(*They watch him. He draws a long breath which shudders down his body. He concentrates.*)

GOLDBERG. Well, Stanley boy, what do you say, eh?

(*They watch. He concentrates. His head lowers, his chin draws into his chest, he crouches.*)

STANLEY. Uh-gughh . . . uh-gughhh . . .

McCANN. What's your opinion, sir?

STANLEY. Caaahhh . . . caaahhh . . .

McCANN. Mr. Webber! What's your opinion?

GOLDBERG. What do you say, Stan? What do you think of the prospect?

McCANN. What's your opinion of the prospect?

(STANLEY's *body shudders, relaxes, his head drops, he becomes still again, stopped.* PETEY *enters from door,* D. R.)

GOLDBERG. Still the same old Stan. Come with us. Come on, boy.

McCANN. Come along with us.

(*They help* STANLEY *out of the chair.*)

PETEY. Where are you taking him?

(*They turn. Silence.*)

GOLDBERG. (*Goes Upstage for hat and briefcase.*) We're taking him to Monty.

PETEY. He can stay here.

GOLDBERG. Don't be silly.

PETEY. We can look after him here.

GOLDBERG. Why do you want to look after him?

PETEY. He's my guest.

GOLDBERG. He needs special treatment.

PETEY. We'll find someone.

GOLDBERG. No. Monty's the best there is. Bring him, McCann.

(GOLDBERG *puts the bowler hat on* STANLEY's *head. They all three move towards the door* U. C.)

PETEY. Leave him alone!

(*They stop.* GOLDBERG *studies him.*)

GOLDBERG. (*Insidiously.*) Why don't you come with us, Mr. Boles?

McCANN. Yes, why don't you come with us?

GOLDBERG. Come with us to Monty. There's plenty of room in the car.

(PETEY *makes no move.* McCANN *opens the door and picks up the suitcases.* GOLDBERG *offers* PETEY *a 5-pound note and then tosses it on the table. They start out.*)

PETEY. (*Broken.*) Stan, don't let them tell you what to do!

(GOLDBERG *looks at him. They exit. Silence.* PETEY *stands. The front DOOR slams.* PETEY *crosses to window. Sounds of a CAR starting. Sounds of a CAR going away. Silence.* PETEY *slowly goes to the table. He puts the note in his pocket. He sits on a chair,* L. *He picks up the paper and opens it. The strips fall to the floor. He looks down at them.* MEG *comes past the window and enters by the front door.* PETEY *studies the front page of the paper.*)

MEG. (*Coming Downstage.*) The car's gone.

PETEY. Yes.

MEG. Have they gone?

PETEY. Yes.

MEG. Won't they be in for lunch?

PETEY. No.

MEG. Oh, what a shame. (*She puts her bag on the table.*) It's hot out. (*She hangs her coat on a hook.*) What are you doing?

PETEY. Reading.

MEG. Is it good?

PETEY. All right.

MEG. (*She sits by the table with darning.*) Where's Stan? (*Pause.*) Is Stan down yet, Petey?

PETEY. No . . . he's . . .

MEG. Is he still in bed?

PETEY. Yes, he's . . . still asleep.

MEG. Still? He'll be late for his breakfast.

PETEY. Let him . . . sleep.

(*Pause.*)

MEG. Wasn't it a lovely party last night?

PETEY. I wasn't there.

MEG. Weren't you?

PETEY. I came in afterwards.

MEG. Oh. (*Pause.*) It was a lovely party. I haven't laughed so much for years. We had dancing and singing. And games. You should have been there.

PETEY. It was good, eh?

(*Pause.*)

MEG. I was the belle of the ball.

PETEY. Were you?

MEG. Oh, yes. They all said I was.

PETEY. I bet you were, too.

MEG. Oh, it's true. I was. (*Pause.*) I know I was.

CURTAIN

PROP LIST

ACT ONE

PRESET

Kitchen:
Hatch closed to within two inches
Shelf under hatch—
  Box of cornflakes
  Bottle of milk almost filled
  2 bowls of cornflakes
  1 empty glass L. of sink
  1 identical glass ¾ full of water
    Towel on hook above R. of shelf
    Clothes line strung across backing with 8 socks and blue
      shirt
    3 dishes in sink
    Round tray with doily and 5 glasses L. of sink
Counter L. of sink—
  2 plates of fried bread with syrup
  Gold tray with:
    Tea pot and cozy
    Tea cup and saucer, strainer in cup
    Tea cup with tea and spoon (Meg)
  Bread and syrup bottle
  Towel on hook above counter
Cupboard against L. wall—
  Assorted groceries and cups and glasses

Living Room:
Sideboard Top—
  Green runner
  Sewing box open with mending . . . threaded needle, R.
  Meg's black purse, L.
  Red birds statuary, L.
Sideboard R. Drawer—
  Sellotape
  Dustcloth
  Clutter
Sideboard L. Drawer—
  Extra silverware
  3 placemats
Sideboard cupboard—
  Bowl of wax fruit

R. of front door—
  Umbrella in stand
L. of front door—
  Mirror with hooks
    U. S. top—Meg's hat and coat
    C. bottom hook—Shopping bag
  On floor below mirror—Meg's tan shoes

Living Room:
  U. C. table—
    Potted plant—heavy foliage facing stairs
    L. of plant 2 rolled newspapers carelessly laid
  Below stairs on floor—
    Pile of British papers and mags messy
    Beach chair folded against wall L.
    Old jacket thrown over stair railing
    Old slacks thrown over beach chair
  Window seat—
    Curtains open
    Batch of pillows strewn across back
    Sweater hanging over edge
    Magazine upstage corner
    Magazine open face down, downstage end
    ½ finished knitting on top R. C.
    Sticking out of seat pair stockings
      Toe out short D.
      Thigh out long U.
  D. L. on floor—
    Shoe box with polishing materials within
    Rag hanging out of locked top
  L. C. Armchair—
    2 cushions
    Messed up antimacassars
    Seat cushion, dirty side up
    Footstool below set so one can pass between
  C. Round table with 2 cloths—
    Arranged in scalloped fashion
    Dundee jar with:
      3 forks
      3 knives
      4 tea spoons
      4 cereal spoons

Sugar bowl with spoon, cracked lid D. S.
3 chairs, S. R. out, other 2 in to table

Doors:
All closed

Prop Table—Off Left:
2 suitcases—McCann
1 briefcase—Goldberg
Groceries—Meg
Drum and sticks boxed and gift wrapped—Lulu
2 flashlights—McCann
4 bottles of Scotch—McCann, in brown paper bag
1 bottle of Irish—McCann, in brown paper bag
String bag with bag of sandwiches and some fruit—Lulu—
   also compact
2 British mirrors (newspapers) Petey (different papers)
Pink purse—Lulu—also in string bag
Brown purse—Lulu
Coin bag—Petey
Ticket machine—Petey
2 rolls of tickets, 1 bigger than the other—Petey
Cardigan—Lulu
Swizzle sticks—McCann
Black Homburg—Goldberg
Prop Table—Off R.:
Gloves—Petey
Drum and sticks

PROP LIST

ACT TWO

PRESET

Kitchen:

Hatch open—Happy Birthday banner over hatch opening
   Shelf under hatch—
      1 glass full of water
      Towel on hook
   Table—
      Round tray with doily and 5 glasses on it
      Towel on hook

Sink—
    In sink 3 dishes
    L. of sink—empty glass
Inside L. of door—
    Meg's purse and shopping bag on hook

Living Room:
Sideboard Top—
    Change cover to lace party cover
    Wax friut in pink bowl C.
Wastebasket—
    Drum wrapping paper in, but sticking out a little (sprayed)
Umbrella stand—
    Umbrella in it
Mirror—
    U. S. top hook—Meg's coat and hat
    D. S. top hook—Petey's hat and sweater
    D. S. lower hook—Petey's ticket machine and leather coiner
U. C. Table—
    Change cover to party cover
    Move rolled newspapers to pile below stairs
Below stairs on floor—
    Newspapers and mags straightened up
    Beach chair remains
Window seat—
    Pillows reshuffled
    Shoe box within seat
    Drummer boy party decoration hung on U. S. end of window
L. C. Armchair—
    1 pillow added (total 3)
    Stool below moved to marks closest to chair
C. Round table—
    Topcover changed to party cover drape rearranged
    Shell ashtray placed on with a bit of water in it
    McCann's large newspaper placed on table
    2 strips of torn newspaper on table
Garden doors both open a bit, D. S. door a little more than
    upstage door

Living Room:
Chandelier—
    Pink fringe added to bottom of it

STRIKE:
  Groceries from Meg's bag in kitchen
  Meg's slippers and curlers
  Drum and sticks. Take strap off drum before placing it on
    prop table, L.
  Sewing box
  Shirt and socks from clothesline
  Old clothes from below stairs go into window seat

Prop Table, L.:
  4 bottles of Scotch—McCann
  1 bottle of Irish—McCann
  Drum and sticks (Strap removed from drum) Meg
  Swizzle stick—McCann
  Cardigan—Lulu
  Brown purse—Lulu
  Homburg—Goldberg

Prop Table, R.:
  Garden gloves—Petey
  Yellow drum and sticks
    (For off-stage drumming during party)

PROP LIST

ACT THREE

PRESET

Kitchen:

  Hatch closed to within 2 inches
  Sink—3 dishes in water
  Table under hatch—
    Gold tray with tea pot and cozy
    2 empty tea cups and saucers
    Strainer resting in 1 of empty cups
    ½ full cup with spoon
    Milk bottle about ½ full
  On drying line—
    wash cloth

Living Room:
  Sideboard Top—
    Change runner back to Act I runner (green)
    Sewing basket with knitting in back to Act I position, top
    leaning on
  Sideboard R. Drawer—
    Garden gloves (dust cloth must be moved free of gloves)
    Cellotape
  Sideboard bottom—
    Broken drum—half on rung, half on floor
  R. of front door—
    Umbrella in stand
  L. of front door—
    Mirror with hooks
      U. S. top hook—Meg's hat and coat
      C. bottom hook—Meg's shopping bag and black purse
  Below mirror on floor
    Meg's tan shoes
  U. C. Table—
    Change cover back to Act I cover
    Potted plant
  Below stairs on floor—
    Pile of newspapers and magazines
    Beach chair remains
  Window seat—
    All pillows returned and rearranged
    Shoe box on window seat with rag hanging out, top locked
  L. C. Armchair—
    All pillows removed
    Stool below on red marks farthest from chair
  C. Round table with two cloths—(cloth has been changed back
    to Act I cloth, and discreetly rearranged)
    3 chairs reset to Act I position
    Dundee jar with silverware
    Sugar bowl with spoon (cracked lid D. S.)
  Doors—
    All closed

STRIKE:
  Ashtray, whiskey bottles, (5) dirty party glasses (5)
  Drum sticks
  Lulu's purse and cardigan

Cornflakes box from kitchen
Birthday party banner
Pink fringe from chandelier
Any broken pieces of drum from within it
Wax fruit and bowl
Drummer boy and all party decorations

Prop Table—Off Left:
Lulu's purse and cardigan
2 suitcases
1 briefcase
Black Homburg
Groceries (must be a box of cornflakes)
Petey's newspaper. (Paper must have a different headline than Act I)
Petey's ticket machine, coin bag, and tickets (smaller roll of tickets)

COSTUME PLOT

PETEY:
Work shoes, work trousers, cap, shirt, old sweater.

GOLDBERG:
Black single-breasted suit, black shoes, black hat, white shirt, dark tie.

McCANN:
Act 1 and 2: Double-breasted tan suit, brown shoes, blue shirt, figured tie.
Act 3: Double-breasted black suit, black shoes, white shirt, maroon tie, black hat throughout.

STANLEY:
Act 1: Old brown shoes, dirty grey trousers, pyjama top.
Act 2: Old brown shoes, dirty grey trousers, pyjama top, old tweed jacket.
Act 3: Single-breasted black suit, bowler hat, white shirt, light grey tie.

LULU:
Act 1: Orange skirt, matching shoes, white blouse.
Act 2: Orange skirt, sleeveless striped jersey top, silk scarf, off white cardigan sweater.

MEG:
Act 1 and 3: Old house dress, apron, coat, hat, red carpet slippers, brown shoes.
Act 2: Old faded party dress, dirty black pumps with pink rosettes.

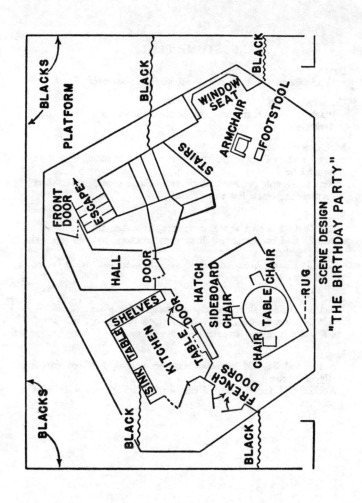

SCENE DESIGN

"THE BIRTHDAY PARTY"

Other Publications for Your Interest

TALKING WITH . . .
(LITTLE THEATRE)
By JANE MARTIN

11 women—Bare stage

Here, at last, is the collection of eleven extraordinary monologues for eleven actresses which had them on their feet cheering at the famed Actors Theatre of Louisville—audiences, critics and, yes, even jaded theatre professionals. The mysteriously pseudonymous Jane Martin is truly a "find", a new writer with a wonderfully idiosyncratic style, whose characters alternately amuse, move and frighten us always, however, speaking to us from the depths of their souls. The characters include a baton twirler who has found God through twirling; a fundamentalist snake handler, an ex-rodeo rider crowded out of the life she has cherished by men in 3-piece suits who want her to dress up "like Minnie damn Mouse in a tutu"; an actress willing to go to any length to get a job; and an old woman who claims she once saw a man with "cerebral walrus" walk into a McDonald's and be healed by a Big Mac. "Eleven female monologues, of which half a dozen verge on brilliance."—London Guardian. "Whoever (Jane Martin) is, she's a writer with an original imagination."—Village Voice. "With Jane Martin, the monologue has taken on a new poetic form, intensive in its method and revelatory in its impact."—Philadelphia Inquirer. "A dramatist with an original voice . . . (these are) tales about enthusiasms that become obsessions, eccentric confessionals that levitate with religious symbolism and gladsome humor."—N.Y. Times. *Talking With* . . . is the 1982 winner of the American Theatre Critics Association Award for Best Regional Play.   (#22009)

HAROLD AND MAUDE
(ADVANCED GROUPS—COMEDY)
By COLIN HIGGINS

9 men, 8 women—Various settings

Yes: *the Harold and Maude!* This is a stage adaptation of the wonderful movie about the suicidal 19 year-old boy who finally learns how to truly *live* when he meets up with that delightfully whacky octogenarian, Maude. Harold is the proverbial Poor Little Rich Kid. His alienation has caused him to attempt suicide several times, though these attempts are more cries for attention than actual attempts. His peculiar attachment to Maude, whom he meets at a funeral (a mutual passion), is what saves him—and what captivates us. This new stage version, a hit in France directed by the internationally-renowned Jean-Louis Barrault, will certainly delight both afficionados of the film and new-comers to the story. "Offbeat upbeat comedy."—Christian Science Monitor.   (#10032)

Other Publications for Your Interest

A WEEKEND NEAR MADISON
(LITTLE THEATRE—COMIC DRAMA)
By KATHLEEN TOLAN

2 men, 3 women—Interior

This recent hit from the famed Actors Theatre of Louisville, a terrific ensemble play about male-female relationships in the 80's, was praised by *Newsweek* as "warm, vital, glowing . . . full of wise ironies and unsentimental hopes". The story concerns a weekend reunion of old college friends now in their early thirties. The occasion is the visit of Vanessa, the queen bee of the group, who is now the leader of a lesbian/feminist rock band. Vanessa arrives at the home of an old friend who is now a psychiatrist hand in hand with her naif-like lover, who also plays in the band. Also on hand are the psychiatrist's wife, a novelist suffering from writer's block; and his brother, who was once Vanessa's lover and who still loves her. In the course of the weekend, Vanessa reveals that she and her lover desperately want to have a child—and she tries to persuade her former male lover to father it, not understanding that he might have some feelings about the whole thing. *Time Magazine* heard "the unmistakable cry of an infant hit . . . Playwright Tolan's work radiates promise and achievement."   (#25051)

PASTORALE
(LITTLE THEATRE—COMEDY)
By DEBORAH EISENBERG

3 men, 4 women—Interior
(plus 1 or 2 bit parts and 3 optional extras)

"Deborah Eisenberg is one of the freshest and funniest voices in some seasons."—Newsweek. Somewhere out in the country Melanie has rented a house and in the living room she, her friend Rachel who came for a weekend but forgets to leave, and their school friend Steve (all in their mid-20s) spend nearly a year meandering through a mental landscape including such concerns as phobias, friendship, work, sex, slovenliness and epistemology. Other people happen by: Steve's young girlfriend Celia, the virtuous and annoying Edie, a man who Melanie has picked up in a bar, and a couple who appear during an intense conversation and observe the sofa is on fire. The lives of the three friends inevitably proceed and eventually draw them, the better prepared perhaps by their months on the sofa, in separate directions. "The most original, funniest new comic voice to be heard in New York theater since Beth Henley's 'Crimes of the Heart.'"—N.Y. Times. "A very funny, stylish comedy."—The New Yorker. "Wacky charm and wayward wit."—New York Magazine. "Delightful."—N.Y. Post. "Uproarious . . . the play is a world unto itself, and it spins."—N.Y. Sunday Times.   (#18016)

Other Publications for Your Interest

HUSBANDRY
(LITTLE THEATRE—DRAMA)

By PATRICK TOVATT

2 men, 2 women—Interior

At its recent world premiere at the famed Actors Theatre of Louisville, this enticing new drama moved an audience of theatre professionals up off their seats and on to their feet to cheer. Mr. Tovatt has given us an insightful drama about what is happening to the small, family farm in America—and what this means for the future of the country. The scene is a farmhouse whose owners are on the verge of losing their farm. They are visited by their son and his wife, who live "only" eight hours' drive away. The son has a good job in the city, and his wife does, too. The son, Harry, is really put on the horns of a dilemma when he realizes that he is his folks' only hope. The old man can't go it alone anymore—and he needs his son. Pulling at him from the other side is his wife, who does not want to leave her job and uproot her family to become a farm wife. *Husbandry*, then, is ultimately about what it means to be a *husband*—both in the farm and in the family sense. *Variety* praised the "delicacy of Tovatt's dialogue", and called the play "a literate exploration of family responsibilities in a mobile society." Said *Time*: "The play simmers so gently for so long, as each potential confrontation is deflected with Chekhovian shrugs and silences, that when it boils into hostility it sears the audience." (#10169)

CLARA'S PLAY
(LITTLE THEATRE—DRAMA)

By JOHN OLIVE

3 men, 1 woman—Exterior

Clara, an aging spinster, lives alone in a remote farmhouse. She is the last surviving member of one of the area's most prominent families. It is summer, 1915. Enter an immigrant, feisty soul named Sverre looking for a few days' work before moving on. But Clara's farm needs more than just a few days' work, and Sverre stays on to help Clara fix up and run the farm. It soon becomes clear unscrupulous local businessmen are bilking Clara out of money and hope to gain control of her property. Sverre agrees to stay on to help Clara keep her family's property. "A story of determination, loyalty. It has more than a measure of love, of resignation, of humor and loyalty."—Chicago Sun-Times. "A playwright of unusual sensitivity in delineating character and exploring human relationships." —Chicago Tribune. "Gracefully-written, with a real sense of place."—Village Voice. A recent success both at Chicago's fine Wisdom Bridge Theatre and at the Great American Play Festival of the world-reknowned Actors Theatre of Louisville; and, on tour, starring Jean Stapleton. (#5076)

Other Publications for Your Interest

SEASCAPE WITH SHARKS AND DANCER
(LITTLE THEATRE—DRAMA)

By DON NIGRO

1 man, 1 woman—Interior

This is a fine new play by an author of great talent and promise. We are very glad to be introducing Mr. Nigro's work to a wide audience with *Seascape With Sharks and Dancer*, which comes directly from a sold-out, critically acclaimed production at the world-famous Oregon Shakespeare Festival. The play is set in a beach bungalow. The young man who lives there has pulled a lost young woman from the ocean. Soon, she finds herself trapped in his life and torn between her need to come to rest somewhere and her certainty that all human relationships turn eventually into nightmares. The struggle between his tolerant and gently ironic approach to life and her strategy of suspicion and attack becomes a kind of war about love and creation which neither can afford to lose. In other words, this is quite an offbeat, wonderful love story. We would like to point out that the play also contains a wealth of excellent *monologue* and *scene material*.   (#21060)

GOD'S SPIES
(COMEDY)

By DON NIGRO

1 man, 2 women—Interior

This is a truly hilarious send-up of ''Christian'' television programming by a talented new playwright of wit and imagination. We are ''on the air'' with one of those talk shows where people are interviewed about their religious conversions, offering testimonials of their faith up to God and the Moral Majority. The first person interview by stalwart Dale Clabby is Calvin Stringer, who discourses on devil worship in popular music. Next comes young Wendy Trumpy, who claims to have talked to God in a belfry. Her testimonial, though, is hardly what Dale expected . . . Published with *Crossing the Bar*.   (#9643)

CROSSING THE BAR
(COMEDY)

By DON NIGRO

1 man, 2 women—Interior

Two women sit in a funeral parlor with the corpse of a recently-deceased loved one, saying things like ''Doesn't he look like himself'', when the corpse sits up, asking for someone named Betty. Who is this Betty, they wonder? God certainly works in mysterious ways . . . Published with *God's Spies*.   (#5935)

Other Publications for Your Interest

SUNDANCE
(ALL GROUPS—COMEDY)
By MEIR Z. RIBALOW

5 men—Simple interior

This new comedy from the author of *Shrunken Heads* is set in a sort of metaphysical wild west saloon. The characters include Hickock, Jessie, the Kid and the inevitable Barkeep. Hickock kills to uphold the law. Jessie kills for pleasure. The Kid kills to bring down The Establishment. What if, wonders the Barkeep, they met up with the Ultimate Killer—who kills for no reason, who kills simply because that's what he does? Enter Sundance. He does not kill to uphold the law, for pleasure, or to make a political statement, or because he had a deprived childhood. And he proceeds to kill everyone, exiting at the end with his sixguns blazing! "Witty, strong, precise, unusually well-written."—The Guardian. "A brilliant piece."—Dublin Evening Press. This co-winner of the 1981 Annual NYC Metropolitan Short Play Festival has been a success in 6 countries!

SEA MARKS
(LITTLE THEATRE—DRAMA)
By GARDNER McKAY

1 man, 1 woman—Unit set

This entrancing play is about Colin Primrose—a simple Irish fisherman with the touch of the poet—and Timothea Styles, a Welsh woman with whom he has fallen in love, and with whom he carries on a courtship via the mails which forms the first half of the play. Timothea persuades Colin to visit her in Liverpool, where she works for a publisher. Timothea, unbeknownst to Colin, had submitted his work to her superiors, who had been entranced by the poetic letters of the Irish "primitive". When they issue them as a volume of poetry, Colin becomes famous. But, because he is a fish out of water, he has no choice but to leave Timothea and go back to the sea, where he belongs. "It's the work of an able writer."—N.Y. Times. "A charming, often wildly and self-consciously romantic play with a great deal of humor."—Newark Star-Ledger. "A tenderly touching and often amusing romantic comedy about an unlikely duo."—Christ. Sci. Mon.

Other Publications for Your Interest

NOISES OFF
(LITTLE THEATRE—FARCE)
By MICHAEL FRAYN

5 men, 4 women—2 Interiors

This wonderful Broadway smash hit is "a farce about farce, taking the clichés of the genre and shaking them inventively through a series of kaleidoscopic patterns. Never missing a trick, it has as its first act a pastiche of traditional farce; as its second, a contemporary variant on the formula; as its third, an elaborate undermining of it. The play opens with a touring company dress-rehearsing 'Nothing On', a conventional farce. Mixing mockery and homage, Frayn heaps into this play-within-a-play a hilarious melee of stock characters and situations. Caricatures—cheery char, outraged wife and squeaky blonde—stampede in and out of doors. Voices rise and trousers fall . . . a farce that makes you think as well as laugh."—London Times Literary Supplement. ". . . as side-splitting a farce as I have seen. Ever? *Ever*."—John Simon, NY Magazine. "The term 'hilarious' must have been coined in the expectation that something on the order of this farce-within-a-farce would eventually come along to justify it."—N.Y. Daily News. "Pure fun."—N.Y. Post. "A joyous and loving reminder that the theatre really does go on, even when the show falls apart."—N.Y. Times.   (#16052)

THE REAL THING
(ADVANCED GROUPS—COMEDY)
By TOM STOPPARD

4 men, 3 women—Various settings

The effervescent Mr. Stoppard has never been more intellectually—and *emotionally*—engaging than in this "backstage" comedy about a famous playwright named Henry Boot whose second wife, played on Broadway to great acclaim by Glenn Close (who won the Tony Award), is trying to merge "worthy causes" (generally a euphemism for left-wing politics) with her art as an actress. She has met a "political prisoner" named Brodie who has been jailed for radical thuggery, and who has written an inept play about how property is theft, about how the State stifles the Rights of The Individual, etc., etc., etc. Henry's wife wants him to make the play work theatrically, which he does after much soul-searching. Eventually, though, he is able to convince his wife that Brodie is emphatically *not* a victim of political repression. He is, in fact, a *thug*. Famed British actor Jeremy Irons triumphed in the Broadway production (Tony Award), which was directed to perfection by none other than Mike Nichols (Tony Award). "So densely and entertainingly packed with wit, ideas and feelings that one visit just won't do . . . Tom Stoppard's most moving play and the most bracing play anyone has written about love and marriage in years."—N.Y. Times. "Shimmering, dazzling theatre, a play of uncommon wit and intelligence which not only thoroughly delights but challenges and illuminates our lives."—WCBS-TV. 1984 Tony Award-Best Play.   (#941)